Storytelling with Children in Crisis

Take Just One Star – How Impoverished Children Heal Through Stories

Molly Salans

Jessica Kingsley Publishers
London and New York

All of the names and circumstances in this book have been changed to protect the identity of Molly Salans' clients. For the same purpose, the name of the town she worked in and the agency she worked for have remained anonymous.

First published in the United Kingdom in 2004
by Jessica Kingsley Publishers Ltd
116 Pentonville Road
London N1 9JB, England
and
29 West 35th Street, 10th fl.
New York, NY 10001-2299, USA

www.jkp.com

Copyright © Molly Salans 2004

Library of Congress Cataloging in Publication Data
A CIP catalog record for this book is available from the Library of Congress

British Library Cataloguing in Publication Data
A CIP catalogue record for this book is available from the British Library

ISBN 1 84310 745 7

Printed and Bound in Great Britain by
Athenaeum Press, Gateshead, Tyne and Wear

Contents

Part Four: The Butterfly

To the parents and children I've met and written about in this book,
who taught me about true hope and how not to give up ever,
To my mother who loves art and children,
To my father who I love unconditionally
And to my daughter Sarah who taught me about unconditional love

Acknowledgements

Many thanks to Robert Smith of Yellow Moon Press who was the first editor to give me encouragement; to Lee Weidman who saw this manuscript at its beginning and whose guidance I could not have done without; to Craig Lambert of Harvard Magazine and esteemed poet Charles Coe for giving me invaluable concrete suggestions, guidance and hope; to Kathryn Roberts, professional editor and writer, whose concrete suggestions, editing, and encouragement helped shape the book into its completed form; to Nancy Brady Cunningham, poet extraordinaire and published author for her undying support and encouragement through the many times I wanted to shelve this book; to Steve Shore, author of *Beyond the Wall* for introducing me to Jessica Kingsley Publishers; to Jessica Kingsley and my wonderful editors, Amy Lankester-Owen and Jane McGill; to Malaena Namias and Debra and Mike Rosenblum for their undying friendship, patience and support; to Jason Shulman, founder of A Society of Souls, and the people I love there, including Arlene Shulman, Michael Young, Kathryn Cameron, Kim Sommers, Brenda Blessings, Ginger Bennett, Martha Harell PhD, Alix Briggs, and Myrna Finn whose Kabbalistic healings, supervision, and teaching has guided me in so many deep personal areas, including to my own place as a writer and to my A Society of Souls class 2002; to my sister, Cindy Salans-Rosenheim, for illustrating the cover of this book and helping a life-dream come true. To all of you, it is impossible to describe the depth of my profound gratitude that I give from the bottom of my heart. Thank you so much.

Stars[1]

O, sweep of stars over Harlem streets,

O, little breath of oblivion that is night,

A city building

To a mother's song.

A city dreaming

to a lullaby. Reach up your hand, dark boy, and take a star.

Out of the little breath of oblivion

that is night

Take just

One star.

Langston Hughes

Introduction

I have the pleasure of presenting this volume of precious stories written from the hearts of children who live in an impoverished area near Boston. Through the use of story and poem in the psychotherapeutic work, these children have slowly begun to understand that the stars, even just one, are theirs to take.

Some of the youngsters in this book have lived in foster homes and all have been reunited with their parents. Some are children of incest, others are children of substance abusers. Some were sexually, physically, and/or emotionally abused. Most have mothers who are survivors of sexual, physical, and/or emotional abuse, and who, despite popular opinion, are struggling to be free of their dependence on public assistance. All of these children witnessed some form of domestic violence; all know of someone who has been killed. Many of their teenage siblings are already parents at the same age their mothers became parents, and very few knew their biological fathers. They all live in communities with run-down schools, overcrowded waiting rooms in medical clinics, streets lined with drug-dealers, and with kindergartners often left home alone in the afternoons to take care of their younger siblings.

In spite of these hardships, the children I met are also full of vigorous energy, often providing hope in circumstances which demand the opposite. The children's names and other pieces of information about them have been changed in order to protect their identities. This book contains their stories, stories which, while they were in therapy, helped them change and validated their hope. While I didn't use the storytelling process with every child, those who did engage in this process were helped. I have not seen some of these children for some time, but it is my hope that they are able to tap into and utilize the memories of these stories in time.

I do not deeply interpret or analyze the stories the children have told me. This book is not about analysis or research. It is about the lives of the children and, in particular, about the way they express their lives through story. At the beginning of each section in this book I describe each child's life in general as well as the therapeutic process through which the stories are told. I include both the tales I told the child as well as his or her stories, written exactly the way they were told to me.

My first opportunity to incorporate story with therapy arose in 1993 through an internship I had at Boston University School of Social Work. There, I facilitated a group for six inner-city girls aged 10–12. At our first meeting they scattered to all corners of the room, pulling each other's hair, fighting, swearing, and spitting. One girl, the largest in size, chose to lie beneath a chair until the group ended, refusing to get up or even move. At the end of that first day I sat crying and exhausted with my supervisor and her supervisor, ready to drop the group or drop school. The head supervisor, understanding my creative talents, suggested I go home and write a fairy tale for each child.

By the next week, I had six fairy tales. I walked into the group, wishing the entire group would disappear. I told the girls I had a surprise for them, had them sit in a circle, and began storytelling. By the end of the first story, one of the girls suggested putting a chair in the middle of the floor. 'This is for the "Queen" of the story. She has to sit here.' Each little monster-girl did turn into a real queen that day. They beamed, they laughed, they added pieces to each other's story. At the end, one girl said, 'I can't believe it – you made us all princesses.' After this experience, the group literally turned itself around, and each girl behaved like the princess in her story. I couldn't wait to do more of this type of work.

In 1994, I began working as a home-based clinician at a state agency. At that time, I was comfortable telling stories, but still unsure how to introduce actual story writing from the client. I decided to stick with what I knew would work: poetry and storytelling. I began this work with Roberto, one of my first clients, a young Hispanic boy aged 12. Roberto was adopted by his grandmother and when I met him, had been expelled from four elementary schools. He had witnessed much domestic violence between his mother and several of her boyfriends, and had suffered physical blows as well.

Our first meeting was in his grandmother's garden on a summer morning. I was impressed that by 10am he was dressed, fed and waiting for me. However, those were the only positive impressions I received. We sat across from each other in silence. He sighed, folded his arms, and looked the other way. Finally, when he would only give yes or no answers to my many questions, I asked him if he would like to hear a story. Since there was no response, and since I enjoy telling stories, I took his silence to mean assent and told him one. While I talked, I noticed that his breathing, focus, and body posture were more attentive. Afterward, when I asked him if he had liked the story, he shrugged in the positive. He remained non-verbal for the next five or six weeks. I continued to tell him stories. By the end of that time, he had attended school for two weeks. His grandmother pulled me aside, and said, 'So far so good, no bad reports from teachers yet.'

'But he's only been in school for two weeks,' I said.

His grandmother interrupted me, 'You don't understand,' she said. 'Usually by the end of the first week he has been suspended for talking back to teachers. Nothing of the kind has been reported so far!'

Amazed, I couldn't wait to see Roberto. We sat outside in the garden in the usual way, across from each other. When I began to tell him another story, Roberto unexpectedly and suddenly interrupted me with, 'Why are you always telling me these stupid stories?!' I was shocked and horrified at first, but then I realized he was actually speaking to me! And so began our first discussion. Roberto's behavior continued to change for the better throughout the year. He had a few squabbles with the teachers, and a few detentions, but nothing compared with past years. It's unclear precisely why Roberto really changed. Being kicked out of several elementary schools, and being removed from your mother's home at such a young age are devastating occurrences. When we met, Roberto's self-esteem was extremely low; he had reached bottom. But he was also an extremely intelligent boy and capable of insight. His grandmother's home was safe, disciplined, and full of love. Here, he had a second chance. He was ready to rise to this new opportunity and make changes. The stories I told him gave him food for thought and more impetus to make those changes.

Roberto's experiences encouraged me. I continued to tell stories to children and families until 1995.

As a result of the storytelling during therapy sessions, most of the time, parents reported small changes in their children's behavior. One client cleaned her room without being told, another received fewer bad teacher reports than normal, yet another went for an entire day without arguing with her parent.

Then, in the spring of 1996, I attended a workshop at a Boston conference held by prize-winning storyteller, Bonnie Greenberg. She taught us a storytelling method, which I modified and describe below. It proved to be invaluable to the creation of the stories included in this book. Ever since that workshop, not only do I continue to tell stories and poems, but I also encourage my clients to tell me their own original stories in a fairy tale form.

With each client I follow a general process, which begins with introducing the elements of a story. The six elements I use are: a good, bad, and helping character, a time and place, and a magical object. When the child is non-verbal or stuck, I help the process by saying: 'The good, bad, and helping character can be any animal or any type of person you wish. For example, you could have a good giraffe, a bad man, and a helping dog.' This helps to tap into the child's excitement and usually the response is immediate. Once they have chosen their characters, I ask the following questions: 'Why is the bad character bad, and the good character good?' I find that once they get going they do not want to stop. When they begin to answer my questions, I write their responses, just as they are told to me.

When the child appears stuck, but still wants to continue after he or she has answered these questions, I ask the following question: 'And then what happened?' Since this is not a creative writing course, I do not ask or insist that the child rewrite or reword stories; once in a while I have changed the tense of the story, but only if the entire story is in one tense, and one sentence stands out because it's in another tense. I then ask the child if he wants to correct this sentence.

The only other thing I change during the process of the telling is the sequence. If a child says: 'and then they stopped fighting forever,' and the next sentence is about more fighting, or how the fighting began to stop, I ask the client, at the very end of the story if I can change the order. This important exercise helps the client put creative thought into order. Those who tell me more than one story often understand a logical sequencing order by the second try. This understanding helps them put all of their thoughts in order – no small thing, given the chaos of their lives.

After the story is told, if they are not too tired, or have not used up the session time, they draw a picture for the story. Or, if time runs out, they draw the picture the following week. While I read their story to them, I will add my own ending. My own ending is written in italics at the end of each story.

Sometimes I elaborate on the endings they created, sometimes I change the endings altogether. Regardless of how I work the endings, I always try to provoke discussion after the telling of the tale. At times a profound discussion arises; at others there is only a shrug of the shoulders. Often, they ask if they can write another story.

After a storytelling sequence is complete, I usually hear from the mother that some behavior has changed for the best, including the fact that the children appear more confident. The most profound change has been in the client–parent relationship. Usually, this relationship is severely strained. Often, the therapeutic storytelling process includes the parents, either directly or indirectly and it has helped the parents come to terms with their own traumatic past, which then helps them make the deeper connections to their children, and their innate love for their children clearly shines through. When this happens, the onslaught of negative criticism diminishes while genuine pride and praise surface. Meanwhile, the children are gaining more self-confidence through both the story writing and the new relationship developing with their parents. This, ultimately, helps my younger clients develop a higher sense of self-esteem, which in turn creates a greater sense of joy and accomplishment.

My clients have clearly over time generated a greater sense of love and hope for themselves.

One issue my colleague and I have pondered over is whether the storytelling process may potentially create more instability and anxiety in their lives by delving deeply into the subconscious of such young clients. The children live in such intense crisis all day long, that when they tell you about monsters, these monsters are not imagined. They are the reality that the children face all day. Indeed, Clarissa Pinkola Estes writes that stories which are 'base can sicken, deteriorate, and anesthetize the psyche.' By contrast, note that the children I work with watch about 25 hours of television a week. The amount of base stories they are receiving is probably far more damaging than the stories that arise in a safe, guided, therapeutic context. 'There is brutality in certain fairy tales…but the context in which fairy tales are told is a teaching, commenting and learning one.' (Estes 1997, p.14) My experience has been this: because of the crises these children live every day, they are already accustomed to the instability of their lives and have adjusted to survive. This, combined with all of the other fictional characters in their lives, adds up to a numbing process, which dangerously narrows the psyche (Estes 1997; Botkins 1997).

The stories my little clients have told me have actually helped to stabilize them and raise their self-esteem. Their entire mood changes in the actual creating of the story, and when I type up the stories with a printed color picture and hand it to the client in the form of a 'book' the result is cathartic and joyous. The child sees his own creativity in a completed form, he remembers its creation, and he usually receives approval from every adult he shows it to, which gives him great pleasure and joy. No parent or child has ever reported a deterioration of behavior or any other serious event due to the actual telling of the story and drawing the picture.

The *context* in which stories and poems are told and created is of the utmost importance. Creating this context allows clients to tap into their innate sense of creativity and to put all of their fears, hurts, and crises into a concrete conceptual place. Their natural ability to visualize is ignited; it is through their fiery imagination that they develop an amazing resilience, a force that enables them to find hope and give joy regardless of how traumatic their lives are.

While you may think that trying to introduce stories and poetry in a mindful way is a hopeless endeavor against the barrage of plastic heroes and real violence in these children's lives, think again. My little clients taught me again and again that their wondrous worlds could be deeply enriched with small, mindful, creative efforts. It has been an honor to be privy to their experiences, and it is my hope that each and every one of them will not only 'reach out' their precious hands and 'take just one star,' but will become the very star that is already shining through them.

Note

1   *Stars* from *The Collected Poems of Langston Hughes* by Langston Hughes, copyright © 1994 by The Estate of Langston Hughes. Used by permission of Alfred A. Knopf, a division of Random House, Inc.

PART ONE

Lady Ragnell

CHAPTER ONE

Moonless Night

Debbie Carlton's house was immaculate; it looked as though no one lived there. Everything sparkled, glistened, and shone, from the chrome on the refrigerator, to the wooden handles on the cabinets. Often when I walked into their home I was struck by the smell of Pine Sol and air-freshener. A string mop, resting in a bucket of water, leaned against the wall, and the chairs were on top of the kitchen table upside down.

I first met Debbie and her family in 1996 and provided individual and family treatment for the next two years. Debbie was ten at the time and was the second to youngest. She was tall for her age, and thin. Her thick, brown hair fell in curls around her shoulders, and her large brown eyes were lined with long, dark lashes.

Both Debbie and her siblings were a great source of aggravation to their mother, Eileen, who worked hard to keep her home clean and her four children organized.

It was difficult to sit in the living room, in spite of the two sofas, as I was afraid to wrinkle a cushion or become a dust culprit. Her children were often such culprits, as Eileen Carlton frequently ran after them, calling them slobs, and yelling whenever they so much as left a crumb behind. In addition, Eileen followed their numerous cats around with a dust buster – cats which Debbie found on the street and adored, and which her mother could not stand, and often attempted to give away. Eileen constantly wiped animal hair off chairs, couches, tables, and counters.

Eileen Carlton's life had been extremely hard since early childhood. Besides being hit often by her mother's various boyfriends, she was neglected and deprived. The many drugs she took as a teenager did not help her situation, probably causing among other things, organic brain disease. Lost and not knowing where to turn, she involved herself with different men who abandoned her. As a result, she was the mother of seven children by the time she was 25; three of these had died in tragic accidents. She spent many of her young adult years with her mother, as her life skills were greatly diminished and she did not have her own apartment, until Debbie was four years old.

When Eileen finally moved her children and herself into their own apartment, she became best friends with Kelley, the neighbor down the street. Kelley was also a single mother whose three children were much younger. Eileen relied on Kelley for many things, including transportation, groceries, parenting skills and, most importantly, 'moral' support. Eileen and Kelley shared the same views about life and, inadvertently, Eileen often sided with Kelley against her own children. The two families often ate dinner with each other and shared in the cooking and the cleaning. Kelley and Eileen's children often played together. In the summer of 1997, at a time when public assistance was forcing single parents to join either a back-to-school or back-to-work program, Eileen was hired to work as a bus monitor 20 hours a week for children with retardation. This was her first job in years and a remarkable accomplishment for Eileen. She relied on Kelley for after-school care.

Debbie and her sisters also had a very difficult time as youngsters. For the first four years of Debbie's life, her family lived with Eileen's mother. The difficulty was that the grandmother did not treat her grandchildren much differently than she had treated her daughter. The unrealistic expectations the grandmother had for her small grandchildren, and her methods of discipline (such as locking Debbie or one of her siblings in a dark room for hours on end), combined with extreme poverty, took its toll on the entire family. Eileen was either unaware of the situation, or completely helpless to change it. Her inability to think a situation through, or to think ahead, seemed to be damaged by the numerous drugs she had taken as a teenager.

The oldest daughter, Connie, was truant, promiscuous, and involved both with the Department of Social Services (DSS) and the Department of Youth Services (DYS). She often ran away, and when she was caught and brought home, she tortured Debbie physically, emotionally, and verbally.

The second sister, Lynn, was shy, obedient, and silent. She often cleaned the house, prepared snacks and took care of the two younger siblings. One day, she too ran away, after smashing her two younger sisters' piggy banks and stealing the little money her mother had in her wallet. Three days later she was discovered in an unsafe neighborhood, and in an apartment kept by men much older than she. Her new apparel suggested that she was ready to engage in posing for pornographic magazines.

The youngest, Billy, swore often, refused to follow direction, yelled frequently at his teachers, and lied constantly.

Throughout the two years I worked with Debbie, she was continually worried and anxious. She spent much time in her room alone talking with herself and her numerous cats. She had trouble focusing on homework and despised the neighbors down the street, 'because they take up so much of my Mom's time. She is always hanging out with them, and she is never at home with us. Then Connie comes home, throws all of my clean clothes on our bedroom floor, wears my clothes without asking, hits me hard in the back, and the shoulders, lights up a cigarette, and tells me if I tell Mom, she'll kill me.' We sat in the kitchen, where there was little privacy, and where we had to speak in whispers, so that a sister or a neighbor would not overhear.

After a month of weekly visits, I asked Eileen if there was a more private space we could use when we met. With surprising understanding, she replied, 'Of course there is. I know that you two need to be alone, and I know how important this is, and here you can meet in my babies' room. You know, I feel they are still with us, so I haven't quite gotten rid of everything. I keep this room locked…it belongs to my three babies. I clean it every day.' When she opened the room, it was even cleaner than the other areas of the house. And on the floor next to the radiator was a bunch of tiny shoes, all lined up in pairs. Eileen then said to us, 'Just sit in here, and if I need you, Deb, I will knock very loudly on the door three times, so you will know it is me!'

In the middle of this session, there were three loud knocks on the door, and Eileen walked in. She carefully placed two steaming cups of hot chocolate on the immaculately dusted dresser near the bed we were sitting on. Debbie's eyes lit up at this gesture and she sipped her hot chocolate joyfully. As she drank, I wondered how I could empower her. Finally, I asked her if she would like to write a story.

'YES!' she exclaimed. She crafted the following story without much help from me. When she finished her story, we talked about the characters.

Figure 1. 'Don't Trust Anyone Evil' by Debbie Carlton

Don't Trust Anyone Evil

by Debbie Carlton

A long time ago, deep, deep in the rainforest, there lived a Princess. She was the most beautiful Princess whoever lived at that time. She was not selfish; she was always kind to her people. If anyone needed help she was always there to help them.

One day an old, old wicked witch, disguised as an old lady, came to the castle to see the Princess. She made sure it was on a day when her parents were not home. After the old lady greeted the Princess, she said, 'You must follow the star that will lead you to the bigger village beyond your own. This necklace will glow when the star is right above your bedroom window; then you must walk down the clouds which sing like steps.'

As if in a trance, the lovely Princess took the necklace. When she went to sleep that night, she stayed up admiring its beauty and rarity, waiting for it to glow brightly. Finally at midnight, the moment arrived. The necklace glistened, and the Princess looked out her bedroom window and saw beautiful-looking clouds. She rose and walked out of her window, down the clouds which sang like the steps, following the star. She was led to an awful-looking village. Here the star stopped glowing and said in an evil voice, 'Come in, my child.'

The young Princess did not know how far she had wandered from her home. A spell had made her walk and walk and walk. And now she still could not help herself. Even though she felt scared, she walked into the evil village.

That old, scrawny witch was standing right in the first doorway of the first house. All of the ladies came out as soon as the old lady blew her whistle and shouted, 'She's here!' Her scream was louder than the morning bells. All of the witches came out to see who was caught this time. They all brought something with them: jewelry boxes, mysterious cups, pots, pans, spoons… The three last witches brought a wand, a huge pot and a spell book. The witch with the wand said, 'Hurry, hurry! Everyone come around.'

Meanwhile, when that horrible witch blew her whistle, the high sound echoed over the Princess's home. The King and Queen woke up screaming and crying. They understood something terrible had happened. They started to search for their daughter. They looked through the whole village. There were no clues to be found. The clouds had gone back to the sky, taking the footprints with them. No one, not even one person, knew where the poor Princess had gone.

The King and Queen finally decided to enter their daughter's very private cave, where the old, powerful Lion slept. He was magical. He could turn himself or others into anything he wanted. Because of this power, he was seldom disturbed. He was there to protect the Princess, who he loved dearly.

When he found out she was missing, he searched his entire cave, but could not find her. He stepped outside, and lifted his mighty head in order to sniff the air. Alas, he could not smell out the evidence; it had all disappeared. But when he put his head down he saw in front of him a tiny jewel that had fallen from the necklace.

When he showed this jewel to the King and Queen, the Queen said, 'I have never seen a jewel like this.' And the King said, 'This does not look like any jewel any villager would wear. This must belong to one of the wicked witches. Oh...our Princess must be with them!'

'Well, you know how wicked witches are,' the Lion said. 'The necklace which this jewel was attached to must have hidden all of the evidence.'

The King and Queen called for all of their knights. They demanded that this noble army be dressed in their heaviest armor and carry their biggest shields and sharpest swords. They were told why they were needed and shown the jewel. All of the knights also knew this jewel to belong to the wicked witches.

Right in the middle of this, a horrible smell started to wind its way into the palace meeting room. The odor from the stew the witches were making was taking over the air. The King and Queen cried, 'Oh no, the witches are making a spell!' Then everyone in the whole village fell asleep, except for the King, Queen, knights, and Lion, who were protected by the Lion's magic.

The Lion helped everyone go to the evil village. But alas, the minute they got there they, too, fell asleep.

The poor Princess, meanwhile, was in the last place of the forest right in the center of the awful smell. Ironically, this place was also quite beautiful. There were rare plants, wonderful tasty fruits, and lots of animals. The Princess was sitting in a chair which had stood in this place for 100 years. The Princess had not fallen asleep yet because she was still wearing the necklace. When the witch who was holding the wand noticed this, she waved it and the necklace fell to pieces on the ground. Then the witch stirring the stew shoved the huge wooden spoon into the Princess's mouth. The Princess struggled and screamed and fell to the ground. All of that noise made the Lion wake up. He followed the echo of the scream all the way to the last place in the forest. He roared at the evil witches and turned them into kittens. When this happened all of the witches died, and the Princess was saved. All of the jewels and riches of the evil village became property of the Princess and her family, who gave generously to their people.

Everyone lived happily ever after, except for the witches, who were dead.

'Who do you know is most like the princess?' I asked.
    'Me! Well…not really…'
    'What do you mean?'
    'Nothing…'
    'Nothing?'

Debbie and her characters

Debbie wanted to be like the princess in her story. She desperately wanted parents who paid attention to her, who would crown her with jewels, and treat her as royalty. She was seeking inner power, much like the lion displayed, to save her from the 'witches' in her life. Perhaps she felt at times like a witch herself, when she argued so much with her mother. Certainly, her stance was like that of the princess, or rather that of a victim, who was waiting for something or someone to save her. In the end the princess was saved by the magical lion, and the evil characters died. Her story's ending indicated that the image of the lion existed within Debbie's own inner life, and that, at least within her unconscious, she did feel she had the power to conquer the 'evil witches' in her life.

Silence.

'My sister is kind of like the witch,' Debbie offered, breaking the silence, 'only I don't want her to die, I just want her to be nice.'

Overall, the characters represented some aspect of Debbie's self. The princess represented Debbie's truer, more generous nature; the witches represented all of the trauma she had internalized, and the queen represented the mother within her. The lion was a symbol of a magician, that spiritual ability to transform trauma into beauty. Somewhere in Debbie's psyche she knew that the mother aspect could not rescue her – that is, the queen in the story could not rescue the princess. The queen fell asleep, allowing the lion to save the princess. The lion had the power to transform the witches into kittens, which in turn both led to the witches' death and the princess's rescue. Debbie understood that she had the inner power to transform her own difficulties. In fact, she wanted her traumatic experiences to die, so that her true nature could thrive. On the surface she wanted her sister to be 'nice' and on a deeper level, she wanted to transform herself altogether.

As I left Debbie's house that afternoon, and drove to my next appointment I was thinking about her story, her difficulties, and the multiple problems that ran in the family. I was trying to understand the family system, and how it worked. For example, it did not appear that Eileen set appropriate limits and consequences for her children. She simply expected them to behave. When she yelled at them, she expected obedience. She did not understand that her own angry behavior created more angry behavior in her children. She did not understand that by taking a part-time job, she was changing the family dynamics. She was no longer around as often. Debbie adored her mother and was craving attention.

However, given the trauma Eileen had experienced throughout her life, it was amazing she was even alive, let alone trying to be a single parent to four difficult children. The part-time job she managed was no small effort. Her ability to be there every morning on time and carry through with her responsibilities without fail was a new and empowering experience for her. Could I help Eileen to change her behavior and also help Debbie stop yelling back at Eileen?

As I pondered this, heading toward my next appointment in bumper-to-bumper traffic on a sweltering hot day in August, I noticed salsa music blaring from open windows of homes and cars. In this neighborhood, many drivers parked their vehicles in the middle of the road while they called to friends standing on sidewalk corners, who were enjoying the heat, smoking their cigarettes. Teenaged parents ran after their children, causing more traffic delays.

As I sat in traffic, my mind wandered to Arturo, my next client. Like the Carltons, there were layers and layers of problems in Arturo's family life. Arturo was a sweet, shy ten-year-old boy who did not talk much. It was difficult to believe that he was actually facing court charges for various criminal acts. I knew his family well, as I had been a therapist for his mother. He lived in a three-family home, on the second floor. It was a three-bedroom apartment where as many as 15 relatives lived at a time.

His mother, Rosa, was beginning to come out of a long depression which had resulted from her own painful childhood. She had witnessed her father's frequent physical abuse of her mother and had turned to drugs and alcohol. She had her first child at age 15 and, with multiple boyfriends, had many more children. Her third child, Jasmina, spent her teenage years in foster care. When I first met Rosa in the summer of 1995, she was struggling with depression, which among other things, kept her from completing projects and maintaining a steady job. She was often restless, and as a result changed her residence six or seven times in the five years that I knew her. These changes were major. She did not simply wander from neighborhood to neighborhood in the same town, but moved from state to state, taking along the five children who still lived with her.

Rosa was worried about many of her eight children. Her two middle daughters, 11-year-old Jessica and 12-year-old Karina, were suffering from bulimia, her oldest daughter was struggling with cocaine addiction, and her son, Arturo, was facing court charges. In addition to her eight children, she had five grandchildren. She was 30 years old.

In spite of the many chairs around the kitchen table, it was difficult to find a place to sit, as books, empty food cartons, and folded clothes took up much of the space. In the kitchen, laundry lines heavy with drying clothes, hung from wall to wall. Dishes, used plastic bags, opened boxes of cookies and cereal, crumbs, and left-over food littered the small kitchen counters, sink, and table. Coats, socks, and sweaters hung over the kitchen chairs. Frequently, when I walked into her home, I was struck by the strong smell of salsa and rice sizzling. Rosa was constantly cooking. At times, she had spurts of inspiration and hope, and these helped her attend a nurses' aid training program provided by public assistance. Rosa found respite in her schoolwork and, with therapeutic intervention, was able to maintain attendance. Due to the fact that she was perpetually moving, however, it took her many years to complete the training.

It was around the time she began her training, in the winter of 1996, that I started work with Arturo. I met with him off and on for two years, and during that period, Rosa moved her family three times. She was a restless woman who hoped that a change of scenery would help her children and herself find better lives. Often the children did not complete their school years, and one of her sons had almost finished high school – he had three months left – when she moved her family out of state. On hearing about this next plan, I spoke with Rosa. She looked at me with sad brown eyes, 'I have to think of my younger ones too, I hear the schools are better in Maine… Juan can finish in Maine.' There was no arguing with her.

In that moment, I felt the family's immense intergenerational struggle around education and successful completion. I understood that for 60 years no one in the family had finished high school. The amount of effort Rosa's children put into academics was tremendous, and I thought of how close Juan was to completing high school – the first in 60 years to do so. Breaking an intergenerational pattern takes an ability to self-differentiate, which involves an enormous emotional effort. The person breaking the pattern (in this case, Rosa's son) must be emotionally strong enough to withstand the pressure that change will cause in the immediate family. If there is no immediate relative to support the family through this change, it is all the more difficult to make, because the process involves so much pain and self-exploration.

Staying wounded or being healed?

When one has been traumatized in multiple ways, as Rosa was, it is, on the surface, easier to maintain the status quo than to begin self-exploration. This process is much like reopening a terrible wound that has never healed properly. The physical reality of reopening the wound, no matter what the result, is difficult to face. Whether one is repairing physical or emotional injuries, there is no guarantee of the outcome. One can only ask, 'Which feels worse right now? Leaving the wound as it is, or reopening it?' In most cases, the answer is a resounding, 'Leave it as it is!' Who actually *wants* to go back and retraumatize themselves? The irony is that reliving the wounds with the conscious purpose of healing them does bring about changes that cannot be imagined before the process occurs.

Doctors, nutritionists, and intuitive healers speak of the mind, body, spirit connection. They talk about healing physical pain by changing thought processes and life-styles. They emphasize the importance of listening to and understanding emotional cues from within the body. The poet Rainer Maria Rilke writes about the need to face grief in order to relive it, as a means to reconnecting to a much more peaceful self. Rilke writes:

Untitled

by Rainer Maria Rilke

It is possible I am inside solid stone, in flint like layers, as the ore lies, alone;
I am such a long way in there is no way through,
and no space; and everything is close to my face,
and everything close to my face is solid stone.
I do not have much knowledge yet in grief –
so this massive darkness makes me feel small.
You be the master; make yourself fierce, break in;
then your great transformation can happen to me
and my great grief cry can happen to you.

We must be able to face our own solid pain and heave a tremendous grief cry as a means of releasing the trauma.

Could I help Rosa to see how important it was to change and to create change gently, slowly, patiently? On one level, Rosa wanted her children to graduate. Jessica and Karina had academic potential, of which Rosa was quite proud. She praised them constantly for their straight-A achievements. They were also involved with peer mediation, the debate team and, at one point, were chosen to participate in a special government-funded college preparatory program. Just as they signed on for this particular program, however, Rosa decided to move.

On another level, Rosa was unaware of her need to keep the status quo. On this level she was afraid of the emotional toll her children's success would take of her. It would remind her of how her three older children, and herself, did not succeed. It would bring to the fore her past: the pregnancies, the drugs, and the repetition of that behavior in her two older daughters.

Rosa would have to dig very deep and review the impact her parents had on her. She would need to re-create the events in such a way as to bring compassion to herself and to those who had hurt her. She would then need to look at how her own parenting had been similar to her mother's and speak with her children about her mistakes. This process, while uncovering much shame, would also heal the dysfunctional patterns and allow more loving ones to develop.

As I worked with the family, I also saw strong, yet hidden, strands of loyalty and love running between and through every single member. I searched for those precious threads, and slowly began to tug.

Arturo's sudden criminal involvement arrested Rosa's ability to move. Perhaps this was Arturo's way of asking for help. He was a special needs student. He held his feelings close to his heart and suffered from sudden, angry outbursts. While he was not a problem child in school, he was failing. His concentration was poor due to the emotional burdens his family carried. Among other things, Jessica and Karina were far more verbal. They were convinced that he was coerced into the criminal acts by adult relatives, and that he was not at fault. Arturo agreed with his sisters through body language or by curt 'yes' and 'no' responses. At times, in their presence, he became more talkative. He was going to face the judge again in another six months. At that time he would be able to give his account of the criminal offenses. It was crucial that he overcome his fear of talking. Therefore, I asked Jessica and Karina to attend the sessions with him.

Often, when I walked into their home, I overheard vicious teasing between the siblings, which erupted into anger and fighting. The comments were endless and so biting, you could almost see bruises underneath their eyes and behind the held-back tears.

I stood in the kitchen for minutes at a time before anyone could hear my greetings. Eventually, the three children gathered at the kitchen table, angry jokes still flying between them. I asked, 'Why are you guys so angry?' And then listened to one complaint after another, sometimes six of them at the same time. I asked Arturo, 'If you saw some guy threatening Jessica or Karina, what would you do?'

'Beat the shit out of him,' this from Jessica.

'Hmmm…so you guys kill each other when you are together, but if a stranger were to hurt one of you, you would kill him instead?'

'Of course,' said Karina. 'You have to stick up for your sister!'

A string of loyalty was emerging. I could hardly grasp it, but I knew it was a thread worth gripping. The story called *Lady Ragnell* came to my mind in that moment. I wondered about this particular tale. It is a story about a heroine, not a hero, and I wasn't sure if Arturo would take to it. I soon realized that girls and women have been listening to stories about heroes for years and years. To tell a young man a tale about a heroine would certainly not harm him and, in fact, may be all the more powerful. How often did he view his own mother as a kind of heroine? And wouldn't this change the entire outlook of the family, if Arturo began to voice his admiration and appreciation for his mother? Wouldn't his sisters benefit from that as well?

Lady Ragnell[1]

A Celtic Tale

This story takes place during the time when King Arthur reigned in England. Many famous knights sat around his round table, including Sir Galahad and Sir Gawain. One night, Sir Gawain and Sir Galahad were riding about the kingdom, making sure everything was safe and quiet. Suddenly they came across a *huge* giant. 'No problem,' said Sir Gawain, as he backed his horse up. Sir Gawain drew his sword and galloped toward the giant. He threw his sword and it landed on the giant's knee. The sword broke into a thousand pieces. Sir Galahad tried to harm the giant as well, and the exact same thing happened: his sword hit the giant's knee, and it too smashed into a thousand pieces.

'What do you want?' shouted Sir Gawain.

'Nothing much,' shouted the giant, 'just the kingdom.'

'Well, you can't have it!'

'I'll tell you what,' said the giant. 'If you can find the answer to a question within one year's time, I leave peacefully, but if you can't find the answer, I win the kingdom.'

'It's a deal,' shouted Sir Galahad, 'What's the question?'

'What is it that every woman truly wants?'

Sir Galahad and Sir Gawain laughed all the way home. Surely Queen Gwenivere, the finest lady in the land, would have the answer!

'Why, everyone wants to be married to King Arthur!' she said.

But that was not the answer. The knights sent a messenger to announce the question to everyone in the kingdom, and the answers came in daily. Each evening, Sir Galahad and Sir Gawain took the bags of answers and read them to the giant. 'Women want fine clothing, women want to own property, women want to marry the fine knights of the kingdom, women want jewels and precious stones…' But none of these was the answer.

Almost an entire year had passed. There were only six weeks left. Sir Galahad was wandering around the river, upset. Suddenly, a frog jumped out of the water. 'Hey, Galahad,' he croaked, 'over here.' Sir Galahad looked down at the frog in surprise.

'I know where you can find the answer to your question.'

'Where?'

'Old Lady Ragnell knows the answer. She lives underneath a tree stump far away. It'll take you three weeks to find her. You have to walk to the end of the forest, walk up and down the mountain, walk to the end of that forest, walk up and down the second mountain, and then walk through the third forest until you come to a large clearing. In the middle of the clearing will be a wide tree stump. Lady Ragnell lives underneath that tree stump. If you jump up and down on the tree stump, she'll hear you and come out.'

Sir Galahad thanked the frog, made some provisions, and hurried on his way. He followed the frog's directions, and three weeks to the day he found the clearing. Sir Galahad jumped up and down on that tree stump for hours. Finally, it creaked and opened. Out from underneath appeared the scrawniest, ugliest, smelliest, most disgusting old lady he had ever seen. She had two long strands of gray hair hanging from a bald head, some hair on her chin, no eyebrows, and her breath smelled so badly that Sir Galahad had to take a few steps back. Even the surrounding trees shrank and withered from her odor.

'Yes…who is bothering me now?'

'It is I, Sir Galahad, at your service.' Sir Galahad bowed. 'I must have the answer to a certain question in order to save King Arthur's kingdom from a giant. And a frog told me you had the answer.'

Lady Ragnell broke into peals of laughter. 'Oh yes,' she cackled, rubbing her hands together, 'I certainly do have the answer. And I will tell it to you on one condition…'

'Anything,' said Sir Galahad.

'You have to marry me!'

The kingdom came before any personal pleasure. Understanding this fully, Sir Galahad consented to marry Lady Ragnell.

Sir Galahad hoisted Lady Ragnell onto his shoulders and carried her all the way back to the kingdom. He arrived just in time. It was one year to the day that the two knights had agreed on their bargain. After making sure that Lady Ragnell was comfortably situated in the castle, Sir Galahad leapt onto his horse, shouting to Sir Gawain to hurry. They galloped to the giant and Sir Galahad yelled the correct answer. The giant had a temper tantrum. He pulled up trees, he stomped and screamed, and ran off crying. 'Oh, how did you ever find my sister? This is not fair, it is just is not fair…' And the giant went away for good.

The next day was the wedding. It was the saddest wedding anyone had ever been to. All of the maidens who had had their hopes set on marrying Sir Galahad were sobbing the hardest, not because they were jealous, but because they could not believe he was marrying someone who looked so unkempt. For walking down that aisle was the ugliest, scrawniest, stinkiest old lady they had ever seen. After the wedding ritual, an enormous banquet was held.

During the feast, Sir Galahad was attentive to his new bride. He constantly offered her one delicious dish after another, and then asked her if she would like seconds. He inquired of her comfort, and wondered frequently if she were enjoying herself, which she was, immensely.

After the long celebration, everyone went home. Soon Sir Galahad was alone with his new bride in their bedroom. She disappeared, 'to change,' she explained. Just as Sir Galahad was beginning to wonder where she had gone, the most beautiful woman appeared right beside him. Sir Galahad jumped out of bed. Bowing to this exquisite woman, he said, 'Pardon me, madam, perhaps you are lost. May I be of some assistance? You see I am a newly married man…' The beautiful maiden interrupted him with lovely laughter. 'Oh, Sir Galahad, don't you see? I am your wife! Why, a witch put a spell on me years ago and the only way I could break the spell was by marrying the handsomest knight in the kingdom!'

Sir Galahad was overjoyed. 'However, my dear husband,' she continued, 'only half of the spell is broken. You see, I could be beautiful by day, and therefore everyone will see what a beauty I really am, and ugly by night, which would bring you so much displeasure – or ugly by day, in which case no one will understand why you married such a woman, and beautiful by night, which indeed would make you happy. So, which do you prefer?'

Sir Galahad being a knight, and already knowing the answer to that precious question, turned to his wife and replied, 'My dear wife, it is my wish to give you exactly what you want. Therefore, I ask you to make this decision.'

'Oh, my husband,' cried Lady Ragnell, 'you have just broken the other half of the spell by giving me what every woman truly wants – the power of choice – and I choose to be beautiful by day and beautiful by night.'

Arturo did not respond to my questions about the story, although his sisters did. When I asked, 'Does anybody in your life remind you of the giant,' both Jessica and Karina said at once, 'Mom's boyfriend. He drinks a lot, and he is mean. He yells at us and tells us to stay in the house or our room, and he stinks. We have no choice. We have to listen to him. Mom tells us to listen to him. We don't have any choice.'

Suddenly, Arturo spoke up. 'We can tell him to leave...all of us. I mean not him, but if all of us tell Mom to get rid of him, she'll have to. We can call the DSS.' In the story, the knights had no luck confronting the giant. When they tried to be rid of him through violent means, their weapons broke into a thousand pieces. Jerry, Rosa's boyfriend, was like the giant. Arturo understood he could not approach him directly. The way to be rid of the giant was through a *woman*. Arturo knew he needed to enlist his mother's wisdom and power. He knew she was under Jerry's spell, and the way to break this spell was through her own sense of wisdom. Once her children expressed their love and concern for her, she could receive her own power, and then make her boyfriend disappear. Arturo understood the choices very well.

I offered help. I told them I would let Mom know about this meeting, and that I would also invite Jasmina, their sister. The children stated they would let their other siblings know, and we agreed on a date and time for the following week.

As I left Arturo's home and drove to my next client, Jasmina, the heat had become worse. My clothing stuck to my skin, and the steering wheel was too hot to touch. My car lacked air-conditioning, and my windows were wide open. The gaseous city air filled my nostrils. As I waited in traffic, I grabbed my water bottle from the small cooler sitting on the passenger seat and drank luke warm liquid. Unexpectedly, a male voice yelled condescendingly at me. The young man was leaning out of his driver's window, and shouting into my passenger window, 'I can't believe you have such a nice car and no air-conditioning!' Unkind laughter followed, and I pretended not to hear. As I inched along, anger bubbled inside the goose bumps rapidly forming on my skin. 'How dare he,' I thought. 'Is there no privacy at all in this town?' Suddenly I saw, through this interaction, the underlying patterns which ran through Arturo and Debbie's families. What I had been seeing up to this point was a lack of boundaries, an invasion of privacy, an inability to respect private space – things I was now experiencing from this driver. I went so far as to wonder if the entire community operated in this manner, and whether this encounter with the driver was a rude gesture meant to harm and frighten, or a normal way of communicating? Which perspective did I choose to see?

Still contemplating this question, I arrived on Johnson Street where Jasmina lived with her three sons. This was one of the worst streets in town.

On last night's evening news, I heard a story about a young mother who lived with her three children on Johnson Street. Her ex-boyfriend, a drug addict with a history of domestic violence, had burst in on her. There had been a restraining order on him, but it had expired the day before. He whipped out a gun and shot her, while her three preschool children watched her die.

On parentified sons

Andy was a very handsome boy who was often put in charge of taking care of his two younger siblings. This is common in families of Puerto Rican and Dominican origins: the oldest boy is expected to carry much of the responsibility. However, for Andy, the role he played in the family was confusing. On the one hand, he was expected to act as an adult. He had to make sure his two younger siblings were awake, on time for school, clothed, groomed, and ready for breakfast. In the afternoon, after school, he was expected to look after them and was often held responsible for any fights or crying bouts that erupted from the two younger ones.

On the other hand, he was a child, and was therefore expected to obey his parents and others in authority, such as teachers, principals, and other adult relatives. If he was giving commands all morning and all afternoon to his younger siblings, why then should he obey commands from his mother? Was he a 'parent' and therefore an equal to his mother? Or was he a 'child' and therefore a peer to his siblings? In addition to this, Andy was confused about moral issues and had a hard time distinguishing right from wrong. Often, he put himself in dangerous situations, lied about them, and became a troublemaker. He fell into a downward spiral of negative attention, which fed into an increasingly negative self-image, and resulted in more dangerous behavior and more negative attention. Mother was constantly yelling and swearing at him and she became more angry when he swore at his younger siblings.

Jasmina and her children were full of the news. Andy (aged seven), Jay (aged five) and Mark (aged three), all leaned out their third-story window and shouted to me, 'Come quick!' They pointed excitedly to the building where the man had shot his girlfriend. No, they didn't know him, but they had often seen the young mother with her children standing at the corner waiting for the school bus. And, no, they hadn't actually seen anything, 'But, boy, were there a lot of police!'

I was there to work with her older son who, according to Jasmina, 'never listens to me.'

Jasmina was also suffering from depression. Her house was cluttered, the dishes unwashed, the clothing strewn about, and left-over food sat on the rickety living room table. Sometimes the phone and electricity worked, and sometimes they didn't. She relied on the children's father – they all had the same one – to take care of these things, which he did sporadically, walking into the apartment unannounced, his arms full of gifts for the children. He was a large man, over six feet tall, with the build of a football player. His skin was a rich coffee black, and he spoke softly, his voice deep. The children couldn't wait to be 'big like Dad,' and they adored him, not realizing just how inconsistent he was both with contact and child support. They loved him because of the gifts he brought, and because of the lack of discipline enforced. He berated Jasmina constantly for the 'filthy house,' her 'hysterical outbursts,' and her inability to 'do anything.'

It was at this point that the state was imposing welfare reform, forcing every single mother on public assistance to join a 'back-to-work, back-to-school program.' Jasmina had just enrolled in school, and she was terrified. Her entire schedule was changing. A woman who was not used to consistency or structure, she was suddenly thrown into a completely new way of thinking and behaving. She needed to find a reliable person to meet her children at the bus each afternoon and had to work through transportation problems. In addition, her time had to be completely reorganized. Jasmina now had to split her time between learning new skills (such as using a computer) completing all of her school assignments, and her children. In addition, she needed to raise her self-confidence in order to achieve any kind of academic success.

As I stated earlier, no one in her family in at least three generations had ever completed high school, let alone college. Even as Jasmina took her first steps, there was no guarantee of success of any kind. However, Rosa, her mother, was under the same welfare reform initiative, and she too had enrolled in training. Rosa's enrollment had a tremendous impact on Jasmina and helped lead to the changes I was waiting for. Suddenly, it was clear to both of them that their struggles were the same. Both were single parents thrown into a whirl of change over which they had no control. If Rosa could succeed, so could Jasmina. I felt I was on firmer ground. I knew that stories could help implement this change. The stories could help Jasmina look at her life and her efforts differently, boosting her self-esteem, which would consequently help her see herself in a more positive light. The effect would eventually help her try new parenting skills as well.

On the day Jasmina signed up for her classes she was excited, and in awe of her mother. 'I can't believe Mom is in fucking training. She really can't help out with the kids. Finally, she has a fucking good excuse! Before she didn't. I mean, you remember how she was always too fucking tired to help me, but then yelled at me for Andy hitting the other grandchildren when I did go over and visit? That's why I fucking stopped seeing her. I couldn't take her fucking yelling. But now it's all different. She's really busting ass, you know what I mean? I even gave her some money to help her with taxis and food, you know, she doesn't have much of either.'

I listened in disbelief. Something wasn't right. Jasmina's phone had been turned off again, this time because her neighbors had run up the phone bill, and hadn't bothered to pay for their calls. Jasmina had asked them to pay several times but they had all moved on, and were no longer in touch. Jasmina shrugged it off as if to say, 'What more can I do, this is life.'

Reexamination: A client's core values

Jasmina and her family caused me to recall the time a stranger commented on my car, and in the process disregarded my 'normal' boundaries. At that time, Jasmina had also told me she was giving, not lending, money to her mother when she didn't have a dime herself. What were the rules in this house, in this family, in this community? Was the ability to disregard boundaries as I knew them – as had been taught to me throughout all of my school training – actually about generosity, compassion, and empathy? The exasperation I was feeling was slowly turning to awe. Was this really poor judgment on Jasmina's part? Or was I watching Jasmina's tremendous natural ability to help and forgive when her family and friends were in need? Was this how she was raised? Was this an outcome of living in poverty and high-crime neighborhoods? How many of us, who are struggling far less, have such an ability? And is this something, in the end, to berate or to honor?

'I can't believe your generosity,' I said. 'I just wish you could give yourself as much as you give to your friends and to your family. Going back to school is going to be good for you – overwhelming, yes, but good. It will show you just how intelligent and how compassionate you are.' The children were listening. They, like their mother, didn't quite understand. Andy, in particular, just looked at me, and stated that he helped his teacher 'all of the time.' Jasmina burst out in a slew of anger, swearing at him for lying again. 'That's a fucking lie. Every fucking day this week I have gotten fucking bad reports from your teacher – how can you fucking even say this?'

'Jasmina,' I said, the patience I had just gained, beginning to wane, 'You have got to stop swearing at Andy. If you want him to stop swearing, you have to as well. Besides which, you yell at Andy more than you do the other children. You have a natural gift for compassion, please use it with Andy.'

Jasmina looked as if she were about to swear at me as well. 'I fucking yell at him, because he fucking lies more than any of the others. He fucking deserves it.'

This was not getting anywhere. Pointing out poor behavior in Jasmina was only creating more defense. The idea of compassion was becoming lost in the mire, and I could only think of one thing to do. 'Would you like to hear a story?' Jasmina settled her sons comfortably next to her, and said, 'Shhh...so we can hear the story.'

I told them the story of Lady Ragnell. Afterwards, the silence in the room was enormous. These children were never quiet, and Jasmina was constantly swearing, yelling, or complaining about something. The absence of their voices was noticeable. Finally, Jasmina said, 'That was fucking neat! I fucking liked that! I liked that she decided for herself. You know, I always make my own fucking decisions, and it's hard, and then their father comes in and tells me I'm doing everything all wrong. I don't know what to fucking do with him.' Jasmina was struggling with many giants in her life – school, her ex-husband, welfare reform, her relationship to her mother. But the entire family, three generations now, had heard the story of Lady Ragnell.

The following week I was on my way to Arturo's house. This was the hour of the great family meeting. I wondered who would show up. I kept remembering the words of a poster that hung on a colleague's wall: 'You mean you want to invite the *whole* family?'

I walked into the small apartment, and Rosa was sitting at her table peeling onions. Jasmina, Jessica, and Yessenia (Rosa's oldest daughter, who was currently in recovery from drug abuse) all walked into the kitchen. Yessenia was nursing her new baby. Her other two children, one aged five, and the other aged three, came running behind her. No one was excluded from the meeting.

I began the session, but Yessenia soon interrupted me. 'Mom, get rid of your no-good, fucking boyfriend.'

'Yeah,' said Jessica. Each child chimed in, voicing their complaints. Tears filled Rosa's eyes. 'You know I love you kids, you know that, and I know that Jerry has been mean to you…'

'He's worse than a giant…' this unexpectedly from Arturo.

'We can call DSS, 'cause Jerry's abusing us…he swears at us…he threatens to hit us…'

'No like him…' this from the three-year-old.

'You have a choice, Mom,' This from Jasmina. 'I mean, look at me – I got rid of dope-head, didn't I?' This was her nickname for her ex-husband.

'Yeah,' Jessica said, 'he's not the man you want to be with. He's got some spell on you…You are always telling us, "Dress respectfully," "Be respectful," "Don't kiss boys or they won't respect you,"' and Jessica walked around the room mimicking her mother, which made everyone laugh. 'No fooling, Mom…just like you tell us we tell you. We want a man who will respect you.'

'Jerry doesn't respect his own ass.' This from Yessenia.

Rosa was in tears. She couldn't believe her family loved her so much, that they would care that much about her welfare, about who she brought into the home.

'You could find someone better, Mom!' This from Karina. 'I get mad when he tells us what to do. He's not our father, but he acts like it. And you just let him do what he feels like...and I hate him. He stinks of beer and he's always drunk.'

Lady Ragnell was working through this family. Even though Rosa had not heard the story, it was being reinvented by her family. They were offering her other choices, comparing Jerry to the giant. They were suggesting she could meet a knight, someone much better than Jerry. They were breaking one half of the spell by helping her see there were better men, by helping her understand that her own parental instruction had found its way into their very being, but that she needed now to follow her own instruction. They were showing her how to do this, they were pulling threads connected to her inner longing, letting her know how much they loved her, telling her how much they hated Jerry. It was up to Rosa now to take their offerings. It was up to her now, to understand that she could break the other half of the spell, by choosing for herself what would be best.

Rosa dissolved into tears. She agreed he was terrible even to her. She told her children she loved them, each one. 'Me too?' asked the three-year-old. Everyone laughed. Rosa picked up her grandchild and hugged him, kept him there in her lap. She agreed to tell Jerry to leave. She took a deep breath. As she exhaled, it seemed that those fragile loving threads connecting each family member suddenly became much stronger. In the end, Rosa finally did kick Jerry out of her life.

Had a spell been broken, or spun? It didn't matter, I thought, as I left their home. The breaking and the spinning of spells was the very essence of story, whether folk or fairy tale, myth or reality.

Note

1 *Lady Ragnell* from *The Maid of the North: Feminist Folk Tales From Around the World*, by Ethel Johnston Phelps (1981). Retold by Molly Salans.

CHAPTER TWO

A Moon Sliver

It was now January 1997. Not a single leaf remained on the few trees lining the streets of this poor town. I was on my way to Debbie's again. She was not doing well. She was not behaving well at home or at school, but she had managed to improve some of her grades.

Right after Christmas break, I began having individual sessions with her at school. The guidance counselor had called and said he was worried. 'Not only was she kicked out of Kelley's house on Christmas day, but she ended up eating Christmas dinner all by herself, in her room at home. On the first day back to school, in the cafeteria during lunch – and I cannot tell you how crowded each lunch time is – Debbie, through a dare, stood on top of a chair and pulled her pants down in front of everyone.'

Debbie did not wish to talk. She wanted to color, she wanted to focus on her cats, and launched immediately into stories about them. I told her we needed to talk about Christmas, about the cafeteria incident. I told her that her guidance counselor had told me everything. Debbie turned red and put her head down to her lap. I asked her if she wanted to write another story, and she shook her head 'no.' I then asked if she would like to hear a story, and she nodded. I decided tell her *Lady Ragnell*. Debbie needed to understand the power of choice. If she understood her choices, and utilized them, she would gain more confidence in herself, her self-esteem would rise, and her grades and motivation would improve. When I was done telling the story, Debbie was completely quiet. I asked her a few questions concerning the message and the characters in the story. However, Debbie did not respond to my questions. I sat in silence with her, at first feeling disappointed that she was so unresponsive. And then I understood that the story I told her had had a powerful emotional effect, that she needed time to allow the meaning of the story to flow through her senses. Debbie had spent many years trying not to feel her feelings, which were submerged deep inside her body, like Lady Ragnell living inside the darkness of the earth. Talking about feelings, even those of the characters, was too great a threat to her.

The story gave Debbie permission to choose her own actions, and she was choosing to be quiet. I had to respect her silence. I did talk to her about the power of choice, that she could choose self-respect if she wished. I also suggested having family meetings with her mom. She beamed at this idea. She promised me she wouldn't 'hurt myself' anymore, meaning she wouldn't humiliate herself in front of others. She said, 'I just wish Mom would cook at home. I just wish we could be a family without Kelley.' As I walked out of the school, I thought about how Debbie would go to any extreme to receive attention. She only knew how to gain attention through negative actions. The intergenerational ties to negative behavior were huge. Was Debbie going to be the one to break this pattern? And was she unconsciously trying to break it by going to an extreme in order to establish new ones? Could story possibly help to implement such change?

That night, as usual, I received a call from the answering service, stating that Eileen Carlton would like a call back 'immediately.' I called Eileen. 'Debbie fucking ran out of Kelley's house swearing bloody murder, and tried to jump out of a fucking window. My oldest daughter is on the run again, and hasn't fucking been to school for an entire week, and my son is facing expulsion and he is only six. What are you fucking going to do about this?' I told her to call the police about her oldest and to call her therapist. I also told her to call the agency and request a therapist for her son, and I explored the possibility of hospitalization for Debbie. Eileen scoffed at the latter idea. I arranged a family meeting the following afternoon. I told her that Debbie adored her, was seeking attention from her, and that somehow things needed to get back on track. Eileen told me I was a 'fucking liar,' because if Debbie really loved her she would behave differently, agreed to the family meeting and slammed the phone down on my ear.

The following afternoon, I sat down in their living room for the family session. Debbie said she was punished and banned from Kelley's house. 'I can't eat there anymore, I can't even go over there, because everyone thinks I hit Kelley's children, but I don't. Kelley expects me to change their diapers, clean her house, and wash all of the dishes. I never get a snack, and because I complain so much and supposedly hit the children, I'm not allowed to be

there, not even to eat with her and my mom. And Mom takes Kelley's side
…says I'm rude and a "effin brat." But I don't care. Mom brings me my
dinner and I sit in my room, and eat with the cats. I share my dinner with
them, because Mom says there's not enough money to buy cat food. She
says she's going to get rid of them, all of them. And what is really bad is,
because Mom works and because Kelley won't take me, I have to go to the
stupid Girls' Club after school, and I don't get home until 8.30 at night.'

Eileen was beside herself with rage. 'How dare Debbie tell such lies! She
does *nothing* at Kelley's, and now because she tells lies about her, Kelley
doesn't want her there. She even picked up the phone to call DSS on Kelley.
Can you believe that? And then she tries to jump out of the fucking window!
And if you would just behave yourself, you could stay at fucking Kelley's,
but you force me to put you in the Girls' Club. The bus ride is free, picks you
up in front of the house, and the only bus home is at night, but you get snack
and dinner, so what are you fucking complaining about…and you don't
fucking get that I have to work and I could lose my fucking job 'cause of
you!'

'I do *everything* at Kelley's, Mom. You're not there. You don't see. I
change Jeff's diapers and I warm his bottles… Kelley makes me do everything…' Debbie was yelling and tears were pouring down her cheeks.

'As I was saying, I don't blame Kelley for worrying, 'cause Debbie could
get her into trouble, like complain to DSS and hurt Kelley bad. The only
reason why she's doing this is because she wants me to quit my job and stay
home with her. Debbie doesn't *want* to eat with us, she asks to leave and to
be alone, and she has to go somewhere, or fucking DSS will be on my case
…'

'I do not want to eat alone…You know very well that Kelley asks me to
leave…and I hate hate HATE the Girls' Club. Why can't we just eat all
together at home?'

'You could eat with all of us instead of fucking disobeying her and me all
of the time. You are asked to leave because you refuse to help her, and you
say, "Fine, I'd rather eat with the cats," and Kelley says "Fine, go eat with the
cats, you're not wanted here." And if you want to call my DSS worker go
ahead! I have enough worries with her sisters, with DYS and DSS in here
every second of the day 'cause her older sister runs away every other
day…and I have to go now.'

Debbie and I walked back into the kitchen, as Eileen had forgotten to unlock the babies' room. Debbie, still crying, immediately started playing with the cats. It didn't matter what the logistics were, I thought to myself, the rift between Debbie and her mother was tremendous, and I knew how much these misunderstandings were hurting both of them.

The power of a mother

A mother's relationship to her child, no matter what the dynamic, can never be underestimated. She is by far the most influential, the most important person in her child's life. Unfortunately, Eileen never understood and experienced this feeling of importance, and was constantly battling in an effort to organize and gain control over her own life. She couldn't see that taking an opposing position in every discussion was actually creating more opposition from her daughter, Debbie. She couldn't see the impact of her own painful past with her own mother on the situation she was now experiencing with Debbie. And she did not realize her own dependent nature as she desperately attached to Kelley, as a means of survival.

I decided to work with Debbie to see if she could let go of some of her own combative attitudes. I began first by letting her know how hard the situation was. 'You don't know how hard.' Debbie cried. 'I just never, ever get to see my Mom. I do everything at Kelley's, but now I'm going to stop. I just get punished all of the time for nothing.' I could feel the tremendous pain underneath these statements. I worried about depression and wondered if hospitalization was needed.

I mentioned, once again, the incident at school, and wondered out loud about Debbie's desperate need for attention. I asked Debbie if she remembered the stories I had told her and the one she told me. I made several references to many of these stories, including *Lady Ragnell*, and spoke about the importance of inner choice. I asked her to think about the things that were causing her sadness and pointed out that when she responded in anger, she was making a choice to fight more with her mother. I used ideas from her own story as well (*Don't Trust Anyone Evil*) and asked her to find that magical powerful lion inside herself. I suggested that she ask *him* to help break the 'fighting spells' that were spinning around her mother and herself. However, Debbie opposed my every suggestion. I addressed that behavior, still talking about the characters she created, when she abruptly said, 'Will you tell me another story?'

I wasn't sure if, in that moment, another story would help. There was enough material with the above-mentioned stories to work with. Debbie probably wanted to change the subject, using storytelling as a means to avoid working on her issues, rather than as a tool to help her. As I was struggling with these thoughts, I suddenly understood how her mother must be feeling.

Power and control battles

At a certain point during my visits to the Carltons, I found that I was in a power and control battle with Debbie. It became apparent that my reluctance to tell her a story, for instance, was directly tied to my underlying wish to 'control' the session, and more importantly, to 'punish' Debbie in some way for opposing me. It became clear then and there that Debbie desperately needed to experience a completely different relationship with an authority figure. If I let go of my need to control in the moment, Debbie would be able to let go of her need to control situations, and then she would be in a position to mirror this relationship with her mother. Perhaps with this method, the depression would lift. Rather than continuing the debate, however, I decided to tell her the following tale, one I had just finished writing.

When Adults Who Weren't Grandmothers Were Too Busy To Answer Questions

by Molly Salans

A long time ago, in the time When Adults Who Weren't Grandmothers Were Too Busy To Answer Questions, lived a little girl named SilverSmart who was unhappy. She was unhappy because she didn't know what she was supposed to believe in.

'Dad,' she asked, 'What do you believe in?' But her father was cleaning the stove and the dishes and the kitchen floor, and his hands and his feet and the stove and the dishes and the kitchen floor were all full of soap. Even his face and his mouth were full of soap, so when he answered, bubbles came out of his mouth, 'Oh, for heavens sake, dear, can't you see I Am Too Busy To Answer Questions?' And he went sliding over the floor to rinse the soap.

SilverSmart went looking for her mother. She found her outside raking leaves, watering the grass, and mowing the lawn all at the same time. The rake was in her mouth, the hose was between her legs, and the lawnmower moved while she sat on it. The little girl ran after her: 'Mom, what do you believe in?'

'Oh, for heaven sakes,' her mother mumbled, for the rake in her mouth made it difficult to talk, 'Can't you see I Am Too Busy To Answer Questions?'

SilverSmart hung her head as she walked away. She walked into the small house where she saw her grandmother Doing Nothing. That is, her grandmother was sitting on a very feathery couch, pulling feathers out of her mouth with one hand, and holding a book in the other. It looked like she was Doing Nothing But Reading.

SilverSmart sat down on the couch next to her grandmother, and feathers spilled all over the bare wood floor. She leaned her head against her grandmother's shoulder; it was full of feathers and sweet grandmother smells. Grandmother stopped pulling feathers out of her mouth and put her arm around SilverSmart: 'What's the matter?'

'I don't know what to believe in. I have nothing to believe in.'

'Oh now, don't be silly,' said her grandmother, 'Tomorrow morning, wake up very early with the sun herself, and go find out what others believe in. Stay away for the whole morning and afternoon, then come back to me when you are done. I will be on this couch with too many feathers, Doing Nothing But Reading.'

The next morning, SilverSmart woke up early and walked outside. The sun was stretching her long rays, and one of them happened to fall on a speck of dew sitting right on top of a blade of grass her mother missed mowing, right there in front of SilverSmart's right baby toe. SilverSmart bent down and asked the dew, 'What do you believe in?' She had to bend down very low and stay quiet for a long time because the dew had a quiet, slow, whispery voice.

'I believe in the Very Early Sunlight and This Blade of Grass, because one makes me shine and the other holds me up,' it said, low and slow and whispery.

'Oh, thank you,' said SilverSmart, and she thought to herself, 'I could believe in the early sun and a blade of grass.'

'Oh, oh.' Just then she saw an ant scurrying out of the blade of grass holding the dew, 'Oh, oh, excuse me little ant, what do you believe in?'

'Work,' said the ant, 'and all of my friends. We all work to find food, we all work to find food. Friends, Food and Work, Friends, Food and Work,' and it scurried away.

'Oh,' thought SilverSmart, 'I would like to believe in friends, food and work.' She continued on her way until lots of white, soft petals fell all over her silver smart hair, face, hands, and skin. 'Oh,' said SilverSmart, 'Oh, you are soft and so beautiful white, and what do you all believe in?'

The petals all spoke together. They sounded like velvet. 'The Wind, the Perfume, and Our Tree, the Wind, the Perfume and Our Tree...' They fell as they sang. They fell onto the dew and drank, and sank into the blades of grass and fell under as food for the ants.

'Oh, oh,' thought SilverSmart (and you know what she thought by now!), 'I would like to believe in our tree, the wind and perfume. Oh yes, that would be lovely.' And then she saw the tree holding thousands of more soft, white blossoms. SilverSmart looked up and down at the tree. 'Oh, blossom tree, what do you believe in?'

'My Roots, the Rain, the Sun, and all of the Bugs and Birds and People that visit me. The roots hold me up, the rain and the sun feed me, and all of the bugs and birds and people keep me from being lonely.'

SilverSmart walked away. 'I should so like to believe in the rain, the sun, and all of the bugs and birds and people, too.'

The sun was rising higher and the rays were warmer. SilverSmart was wanting to believe in so much that she was becoming sleepy. She came to the pond. There were lots of ducks and geese, and all kinds of birds floating on the water – paddling, flying, playing great flying chase games with each other beneath the high clouds. She sat next to a duck: 'What do you believe in?'

'Flying and Floating and Squawking and Squatting, Playing Chase and Catching Fish.' He shook his bright green feathers and said, 'Excuse me a moment.'

'Flying and floating and squawking and squatting, playing chase and catching fish,' repeated SilverSmart to herself. She was sitting near the edge of the pond and watched the water lap gently just below her feet. It never sat still long enough for her to ask her question. So she sat silently, and asked first the ripples, and then the entire pond what it believed in. The answer was in the rhythm of the water. 'The Winter Ice, the Spring Melting Sun, the Blowing Wind, and the Fish I hold, the Weeds and their Seeds, and the Families who come to sit, the Birds that float and paddle and those that fly. They all make me glow and flow, wave and lap, rise and fall, all make me glow and flow, wave and lap, rise and fall.'

'Oh,' said SilverSmart, and she was yawning, 'I think I must sleep.' She spread herself out on the warm grass and closed her eyes. 'What do you believe in?' sang into her day sleep. The dew on the blade of grass, the ant going to work, the velvet blossoms, the fine tree, the ducks and the geese, the birds flying and chasing, squatting and squawking, the pond with its singing, and the reeds and weeds – all seeded songs in her day sleep.

When SilverSmart woke, the sun's rays were shrinking, and everything was beginning to glisten with evening light. She rose and walked home. As she walked, she sang, 'What do I believe in?' and when she arrived home, the grass was perfectly raked and mowed, and the kitchen was glistening clean. Her parents were sound asleep because they lived in a time when Adults Who Weren't Grand-mothers Were Too Busy To Answer Questions. She found her grandmother on the too-feathery couch. With one hand she was pulling feathers out of her mouth, and with the other hand she was holding a book and Doing Nothing But Reading. She was wide awake. SilverSmart sat down next to her.

'What do you believe in?' her grandmother asked, putting her arm around SilverSmart. 'I believe in dew, and blades of grass, and ants that work for food and friends. I believe in velvety flying petals all white and not silver at all, and blossom trees that hold birds and bugs and love people visiting. I believe in ducks that squawk and squat and fly and chase their bird friends, the winter ice and spring sun melting on the pond which holds many fish and weeds and seeds.' SilverSmart put her head down on her grandmother's shoulder, which was soft with feathers and grandmother smells. 'I believe I can make this a song…I believe I can…' and her sleepy words fell into grandmother hugs. And her grandmother spoke like the wind carrying velvety petals, and her sounds landed like dew all shiny on SilverSmart's sleepy silver face. Still singing, her grandmother walked SilverSmart to her little comfortable room, and lifted her onto her bed. She covered SilverSmart with cozy sheets and a warm comforter and sat down next to her, stroking her silver hair.

'Yes, SilverSmart, sing and grow wings. When a question, a poem, a song enters your bones, you will be carried along…wavy colors and strange birds, shining lines and colorful words, with a question, a poem, a song, your thoughts will grow and flow long…'

And the ant tucked himself beneath the blade of grass after a long day's work. The sun gathered in her rays for the moon to begin. Petals settled on the branches waving gentle lullaby night waves, and the pond lapped rhythms to her geese and ducks tucked inside their feathers. All of them asleep along the grass. While her grandmother sang, her hands fell like feathers on SilverSmart's hair, and SilverSmart joined the drifting animals sifting through her night dreams full of grandmother songs.

I had barely finished telling this story when I heard Debbie laugh and say, 'I believe in my cats!' And then she unexpectedly said, 'I wish I had a grandmother like that… Can I write a story now?'

I followed Debbie's direction, not wanting to push this first hint at disclosure. The stories were reminding her of things, stirring images and feelings, slowly simmering their way through her body and thoughts. She was identifying with SilverSmart, afoot on a similar journey, looking for faith and belief. Direct questions would bring the memories to the surface too quickly, and she would not be prepared to handle them. A slow steaming process was necessary, and the perfect spice was, of course, something of her own creation. Debbie told me her second story, *The Cat Princess*. It took her two sessions to complete.

The Cat Princess

by Debbie Carlton

The day I got Cookie, she was lost in the woods. Cookie was a small, little kitten who was lost. When I brought her into my room in the palace, I gave her a big bowl of milk. She drank all the milk and went to sleep as I pet her.

After a couple of days, she met Whacko. Whacko was Queen of the Cat Palace. The Cat Palace was a little castle made for cats. It was in the living room of my palace. When Cookie saw all the other cats, her tail stood on end and she hissed. Then she growled and meowed and ran away outside to the backyard.

She lay by this big, beautiful apple tree. She started purring as she went to sleep. And soon, after a while, I came outside to see where she went. She was right by the apple tree falling asleep. I started to pet her and told her not to worry. All she did was get up and do poop. Then she came over to me and started cuddling around my legs. I told her she would make a great princess and a great kitty if she had a bath. A few minutes later, I took her in and gave her a nice big bubble bath. After struggling with that cat for a few hours to give her a bath, she was nice and wet and all washed up. I dried her off with a towel and dry-blowed and combed her down with one of the brushes I bought her. Soon she looked like a beautiful Money Cat.

I bought her a nice cat bed so she would stop hogging my bed. It took her a few days to get used to her own bed, and she didn't like the other cats that much.

One day, the Royal Queen Whacko came into my bedroom. She called on Cookie and said, 'Once you do the right thing, you will fully become a princess. You must love the blades of grass, the other cats, the ponds and animals around you. You must care for the flowers as well as the blossoms. And you must come to the palace and you will have a home. There my dear, you will get your crown. Someday you will be happily married and made a queen. Then you will have a castle of your own. You must meet all the other cats right now. As soon as you see them, you will be able to speak as the sun sets over thee. And then you will speak and that's how you learn how to talk. You'll be just fine and okay.'

'The very next day, in you will move, and in you will stay. You will learn how to take baths like the rest of us and above this beautiful, beautiful ground tomorrow you will get your first crown. And then you will act as a princess but not as a queen. Now, you come with me.'

Cookie followed Whacko very nervously and by the time they got into the Cat Palace the sun set over them. When Cookie met all the other cats, she was struck into surprise. She had a beautiful voice, and she could speak! She met all the cats of the Cat Palace and learned the royalty of the Queen.

That night she climbed the royal tree where the moon could tickle thee. After a while she left the tree and said goodbye to the moon. She curled around the tree and said, 'Thank you.' The tree gave her blossoms right by her ears and pet her three times and said, 'You're welcome.' And then she left for the inside of the palace. She had her dinner and went to bed.

In the middle of the night she got up out of bed and went to the beautiful pond in the big backyard. She was singing a beautiful song to use her voice a little bit, as the small soft winds blew within the blades of grass growing from the ground, and as the petals blew all around and flowers bloomed from site to site and beautiful perfumes of the night were all around.

The evil cat came out of the darkness of the night. She walked over to Cookie right in front of her sight. Cookie stopped singing in such a fright that she jumped back frighteningly, as the evil cat said, 'Don't be afraid, my dear. I used to be one of you too. I used to be a princess until I betrayed my own friends.'

Cookie said, 'Where's your crown and what did you do?'

The evil cat said, 'My crown has been taken away because I am not loyal and I am not honest. And for years I have always wanted to be the Big Queen until one day I was made to live in the Cat Palace. I had to take baths and become the Rightful Princess. But one day, I saw a witch, and she said, "I will make you a potion which will make you the Big Queen. You could take over some humans but not too many. They will respect you as the Beautiful Queen." I knew better than to trust the evil witch, because I was warned about her, but yet I did not listen.'

Cookie asked, 'Why didn't you listen?'

The evil cat said, 'Because I wanted so much for myself and not for anyone else.'

'Couldn't you have at least thought about what you were doing first?' Cookie asked.

'Not quite. I was still young, and decisions are rough when you are young. It is beautiful here, but I know of a place which is more beautiful.'

Cookie said, 'How far is it?'

'Not too far. It's a part of the yard you haven't seen yet.'

Cookie said, 'All right, but I still don't trust you at all.'

The evil cat said, 'If you don't want to come, you don't have to.'

Cookie said, 'How come you keep giving me a choice? Don't you want to be young again?'

'Yes,' said the cat, 'but the magic is way too powerful to ever break.'

Cookie said, 'Fine, I will come with you.' And they both walked slowly into the night.

Soon the evil cat disappeared. Cookie was all alone. But yet she heard the cries of some small little babies. She walked over to a little hill and she saw a bunch of baby kittens. They were real, real, real, young and Cookie asked, 'Where's your mother?'

'We don't have one,' a little kitten said. 'She died this morning.'

Cookie said, 'Then who will take care of you?'

The kitten said, 'We don't know.'

Cookie said, 'You will need a home immediately.' Cookie carried the kittens one by one back and forth into the castle. At last she had all 16 of them inside. She started to call the other cats. Soon Queen Whacko came out.

'What is it, Princess Cookie?'

'There are 16 young kittens without a mother. What are we to do?'

'You are to love them and care for them as if they were your own.'

Cookie said, 'Fine with me.'

That night, Cookie was busy with all the little kittens. The eight girls wore beautiful ribbons and bows, and the handsome little boys wore little ties.

Then she made a nice bed for the little ones. She lay down in it and the little ones lay right next to her. Soon Cookie and the kittens woke up. The sun was shining beautifully. They could hear the birds singing happily all around. The little kittens whispered, 'What's that, Mommy, what's that?'

'Cookie said, 'Just the birds singing.'

The little kittens whispered, 'We're hungry, we're hungry.'

Cookie said, 'I'll get you some nice warm milk in a minute.' Cookie went out and brought some milk. It was all nice and warm for the little kittens to drink. She got some cream and a few little pieces of fish, and the kittens and she ate breakfast together. Then she gave them a nice big bubble bath and, of course, she went in there with them. The little kittens bounced on the bubbles and played around in the tub.

Soon Cookie let the kittens play in the tub while she cleaned herself. Then, when they were done they all got nice and dry. The girls had their hair put up in ribbons with beautiful bows. The boys got their nice little ties. Their hair was combed down just enough to make them look like little gentlemen.

Cookie put on her necklace. 'I'm going to freshen up. You little ones stay right here and I will get you some toys.' She brought them a toy mouse and a couple of balls. The kittens played and played while Cookie freshened up in the mirror.

When Cookie was done, they all brushed their teeth. Cookie said, 'Let's go outside.'

When they were outside, Queen Whacko was there along with everyone else, holding Cookie's crown on a red pillow. Whacko said,

'You know that old witch cat? That was me! But a young cat did die that very morning and those were her young babies... You are now a queen and you should still take care of those kittens too.'

Little Space put the crown on Cookie's head and Cookie said, 'I will always take care of these kittens.' Then Little Space joined the games with the little ones.

From that day on, there has always been queen and king cats from the Old Cat Palace.

The moral is: In order to be something, you must give trust, be fair, and care about everything.

After the second session and completion of *The Cat Princess*, I asked Debbie more questions. 'Most of the cats in this story are so nurturing...and those poor abandoned kittens! Do any of the cats or kittens remind you of anyone you know?'

'Not really.'

'This story tells me that you must really know how to take care of young things, kittens, babies...'

'My mom really misses her babies. I wish they hadn't died.' There was a long silence.

'My grandmother was so mean. You would not believe the things she did.' Debbie began to tell me some things about her past that day. Terrible things like being locked in a closet for hours on end, being hit and yelled at. She was identifying with her story, with the abandoned kittens, with the princess who nurtured them and with the evil cat who wanted everything for herself. Listening to stories and telling her own was beginning to have a profound effect on Debbie. Already her grades were improving, and in this session she felt safe enough to speak about her past trauma, in a way she never had before.

On my way to Jasmina's, I was feeling hopeful. I walked into her home, only to find her more irate and confused than ever. Jasmina was actually in college, completing her assignments and receiving straight As. Although she had ironed out all of the logistics for school, she was still having a hard time adjusting to the demanding new schedule. Her finances had reached an all-time low, and she was facing eviction. The only home offered to her was her mother's, and Andy's behavior was becoming worse.

Intergenerational anger and love

Debbie was desperate for her mother's attention and, at the same time, she was exhibiting a great ability to take care of others. The roles she was playing in her family were confusing and deeply upsetting her. Her own mother, unable to meet Debbie's emotional needs, because her own emotions were not nurtured, was unconsciously meeting these emotional needs with anger. Debbie's grandmother met Eileen's emotions with anger, and so Eileen was meeting her childrens' needs in the same way. Through this passed-down behavior, Debbie was also learning to meet emotional needs with anger. It was the way to connect to those she loved. However, Debbie also had an ability to nurture. She was overly concerned about Kelley's children, and often talked about her caretaking role, real or imagined, as if she were their mother. Debbie was clearly struggling with the very issues described in her story. Which role should she choose, and at what given moment should she choose these roles? The evil queen, wanting everything for herself; the abandoned kitten, who will eventually be rescued by a loving caretaker; or the loving caretaker who is rewarded with a royal crown? In any case, as in *Don't Trust Anyone Evil*, good triumphs over evil. And, like her other story, I knew by this ending that deep in Debbie's unconscious life she was working toward such an end.

'He fucking brought a knife to school and chased another first grader, he's fucking facing expulsion! Get out of my sight!' she yelled at him. I followed Andy into his bedroom, one which he shared with the other boys. He threw clothes, papers, books, paper cups, and plates onto the floor in order to make room for us. He shut the door, and we both hoped we would not be interrupted. Andy hung his head, his long hair falling across his face. His feet dangled over the bedside, barely touching the floor. He looked so small, so estranged. 'What happened?' I asked. He shrugged his shoulders, still looking at the floor. 'Did you chase another kid with a knife?'

'I didn't. I found the knife. An older kid was chasing me. Then I found the knife and I wanted to get him back.'

This didn't sound feasible. And Andy was scared. Anything I asked, anything we spoke about, did not get us any closer to resolution. I told him the story of *When Adults Who Weren't Grandmothers Were Too Busy To Answer Questions*. He told me it was a 'nice story,' and he was quiet. I let the rhythm and words wash over, rock, and soothe him. His breathing became deeper, and his body was less rigid. After a few moments, I asked if he would like to write his own story.

He suddenly looked at me, his large brown eyes filled with tears. 'Yes.' Andy told me the following story.

Figure 2. 'The Old Lady Who Lived in the Forest' by Andy Berto

The Old Lady who Lived in the Forest

by Andy Berto

A long time ago there was an old lady who lived in the forest. She knew lots of things, like magic and how to fly. She knew a lot because she often thought about things, like how you should never kill anybody.

She thought that if she killed one person, then that person would never see his family again and the family would miss the person who was killed. She knew that she could get arrested for killing, and she knew for a fact she didn't want to be in prison, not even for one day. Instead of killing, she helped the people. She could cure sick people and sometimes bring the dead back to life.

The Zebra lived near the old lady. He was always jumping on her trying to hurt her and kill her. He didn't want to be doing these hurtful things to her. A demon was making him do them.

One day, early in the morning, the old lady had just woke up. The Zebra broke down her door. He jumped on the old lady and said to himself, 'You bad demon.'

Right then, the old man who lived next door to the old lady, suddenly came into the room. The old lady was his best friend. He wanted her alive; he wanted her to live forever. He was mad when he saw the Zebra on top of his friend.

The Zebra had never seen the old man so mad. He burrowed his eyebrow, he clenched his fists. In a very quiet voice, he said, 'Get out.'

The Zebra ran out fast. The scared demon followed, and he never came back. Then the old lady and the old man stayed alive forever and ever.

The old lady continued to do her work of thinking about things and helping others for a very long time after that, and no one was happier than her best friend, the old man.

While Andy was telling this story, the atmosphere in the room became less oppressive. He held his head up the entire time, and kept jumping when he thought of the next sentence or idea. The title and the old lady in the story were reminiscent of *Lady Ragnell*. The relationship between the old man and the old lady was much like the relationship between the grandmother and SilverSmart.

Andy spoke about the characters, stating that he felt sad because the old lady almost died, and 'I didn't want her to die.'

Throughout the rest of the session, he continued to relate to his own characters. I mentioned ideas in the story I had just told, bringing in the idea of inner faith and imagination, as well as ideas from *Lady Ragnell*, and reintroducing the idea of choice. I let him know that he could choose to be any character he wanted. He didn't always have to be the zebra. He could be like the old lady or the old man. He could bring his own understandings of faith and imagination to his life now.

Just before I left, I spoke with Jasmina, encouraging her to keep a stricter eye on him. The stories, I knew, were helping. 'Just remember that story about Lady Ragnell,' I told her. 'The possibilities of choice are endless. You could choose to be kinder to him, to at least stop swearing.' But I saw Jasmina turn her back. Lecturing never helped. 'Next time I come,' I said, 'I'll tell you another story.'

I drove away thinking that no matter how chaotic life was, stories helped to implement order. I found myself inducted into Andy's story as much as he had been. When he was creating *The Old Lady who Lived in the Forest*, I was pulled immediately into the process, and the story. Was Andy psychotic and hearing voices? Is that what the zebra symbolized? I shook my head. He wasn't psychotic. He was struggling with harsh issues, trying to make sense of his poor behavior, much in the way the zebra tried. For in the very moment that the zebra attacked the old woman, it appeared that he (the zebra) did not want to be doing this. He reacted as though a 'bad demon' were forcing him to behave in this way. And when the zebra finally left, he took the bad demon with him. What was causing Andy to act as though there was a 'bad demon' inside of him? All of the confusion at home, the yelling and swearing from Mom, the expectations she had of him, the absence of a father, and the poverty and disorganization. Wouldn't this make any young child angry enough to pick up a knife? Could stories then infuse morality into Andy?

Transformed through story

Elissa Pearmain, a storyteller, educator, therapist and dancer says: 'We relate to story in part because its basic, almost universal structure mirrors our experience of being human...we are naturally interested in the story of how others transform because they provide clues for our own life journey. And conversely, when we tell a story using the images in our own hearts, we tell others about the experiences we are having, or had, and through the creating and telling of our own story we bring to life and creatively change those elements we think need changing within ourselves.' (Pearmain 1999, p.x)

Arturo had done a tremendous job at the family meeting a few months before. While he was now becoming somewhat more expressive, he was still having enormous difficulty discussing his court charges as he kept thinking about his choices. He was going to court in just two more weeks, and he was expected to face the judge with an explanation of his charges. He was in desperate need of preparation.

The power of change

When Rosa's children begged her to ask her boyfriend to leave, she responded by kicking him out of the house and finding a different boyfriend whom all of the children liked. This had a huge impact on the family because it was a direct response to the children's pleas, indicating that Rosa took their pain to heart. They understood from her action that they were valued by her, and in return, very slowly, the way ice melts on a river, the love and respect they felt for their mother was flowing back toward her. As a result, even the children's fighting among themselves was diminishing. They found invaluable empowerment through their teamwork. And this teamwork penetrated deep into their every cell, changing ever so slowly their boiling point with each other. Something bound them, something positive and powerful, instead of the usual anxiety and negative attacks.

I remembered thinking months before that there was deep loyalty in this family, and all that I had to do was find the threads. Remembering this faith now, I knew that Arturo would be able to express himself appropriately in front of the judge. I already knew how much stories were feeding him. I had told him many by now, including the one with SilverSmart.

I mentioned the story in our session. We were alone. His sisters were out and about. I told him that, like SilverSmart, he just needed to have faith in his own self-expression. If he could remember how he stood up in that family meeting, he could stand up for himself, calling on his belief in his own strength and creativity to pull himself through. We tried role-playing, thinking up different things he could say to the judge, but Arturo couldn't participate. I ended up being the judge and my client. I played both parts, and watched his face burn red as I mentioned all of the things he had been accused of. I recognized that Arturo was feeling deep shame for his behavior. This was shame he had to face within himself and talk about. I mentioned this to him, and he hung his burning face so far down, that I thought he would set fire to his own body. I knew I had to guide him down into this shame and out again so he could find the courage to speak to the judge. I told him the following Celtic story. Before doing so, I explained that the faerie folk in Irish myth were very different from the helpful fairies in *Cinderella*. I told him that they were cruel and terrible, and lived in foggy, misty moors in Ireland, far away. Why, I told him, if the faerie people should capture you, don't ever eat or drink at their banquet table. As scrumptious as the food may look, and as hungry as you may feel, you will be eating poison, and then you will lose yourself in their land, unable to return, unless you remember to leave the table and face the faerie queen. For one hour of faerie time is worth days of human life, and the poisonous food makes you lose your own reasoning faster than anything. It is best to hold your own counsel at all times and confront the faerie queen as soon as possible. In this way you can escape much sooner. I told the following story.

A Fair Exchange[1]
A Celtic Tale

A long time ago, in a small village in Ireland, lived a young lass named Deirdre who was all alone in the world except for her baby girl, Gwendelon. Deirdre lived in a tiny cottage, and she didn't have much except a cow and a small plot of land her parents had left her, before they died of illness. The lass milked the cow daily, and pulled tomatoes and potatoes from her land, and she earned a meager living from working in the fields.

On the morning this story begins, Deirdre, as usual had risen early, picked up her baby, and walked down to the fields where she worked all day. Once she had fed her, Deirdre wrapped a blanket around her plump, black-haired, pink-cheeked baby and placed her underneath a tree. Then she picked up her hoe and started work across the fields.

When she was halfway down the rows, she heard Gwendelon crying. 'Strange,' she thought to herself, 'that cry is strange. I wonder if my darling is sick?' Deirdre ran back to her baby and picked her up, for she was wailing loudly. However, when Deirdre unwrapped the blanket, she let out a gasp. Inside the woolen cloth was a pale, thin, red-haired baby boy! Why, it looked unearthly. And suddenly Deirdre knew that the faeries had come, taken her beloved Gwendelon, and put one of their changelings in her place! The baby was crying so, that the lass fed him. How could she not? At the end of the day, she picked up the changeling and brought him home with her.

That evening, Deirdre walked up and down her village, holding the changeling, asking everyone she met if they had seen her baby. No one had. She was told to leave the baby alone in the cold. He would die, and her baby would be returned at his death. The advice was too horrible to consider.

A few months passed. It was almost Halloween. The young lass had been taking care of the changeling, and he was growing. He was less pale and more plump but, oh, how Deirdre missed her own! One crisp October morning, when the leaves were so orange one thought they might set fire to the trees, the young lass went to the market place. She had the changeling with her, and as usual asked everyone she met how she might get her daughter back. A woman there finally told her about the old woman who lived out on the moors. 'She lives mighty far, but she is a faerie expert. Why, her home is not far from their mound. She can tell you what to do if anyone can!'

Deirdre listened carefully to the directions, and the next morning she woke early, dressed and wrapped the changeling, and set off for the old lady's home. It was a long way and the wind was biting; the air chilled her bones. The leaves in their mighty colors fell continuously, and the ground crunched beneath her feet. It was almost dark when the young lass arrived, and the old lady, though not surprised to have a visitor, was not terribly kind either. Of course, she welcomed the lass, and gave her delicious soup and warm bread, but when she heard why Deirdre had come, she shook her head, and sharpened her tone of voice.

'Ay, lass, give up...don't greet the faeries. Get rid of the change-ling as they have told you.'

'Oh, I could never do that. And I must have my baby, I must. I have been told that you know how to do this, and I have come such a long way. You must help me.'

'Don't you know, lass, that you must face the faerie queen? And don't you know that if you speak with her, she can play with your thoughts and make you mad for life – or worse, she can capture you and take you to her faerie land, from where there is no escaping?'

Deirdre shook her head. 'I don't care. I don't mind the danger. Oh, please help me. I will face her at any cost!'

The old woman was impressed with the lass's courage. 'Well,' she said, after a silence, 'this is what you must do. You must offer the queen a fair exchange. A bargain, you see? The faeiries cannot help how they are, for they are born without hearts. Therefore you must never let the queen know how much you want your baby back. A fair exchange is what you ask for. You give her back her changeling, and she gives you back your baby. Nothing more and nothing less. Do you understand? The faerie queen comes out of her mound on Halloween at midnight. You can go to her mound, which is just over there and wait.' The old woman pointed out her window. 'The minute she leaves her mound, you stop her, and let her know your business.'

'Oh, thank you,' said the lass. 'I will do just that.' Deirdre took her leave and walked over to the mound. She poked about, hoping against hope she would find the opening to the mound then and there. But it was dark, and very cold. Deirdre started on her way home, and did not arrive until daybreak. When she arrived, she fed the changeling, picked up her hoe, and headed out for a long day's work in the fields.

On the morning of Halloween, Deirdre woke early, and as before, wrapped the changeling well. She packed what little food she had, and started out, excited to have her daughter back again. But the winds were terrible, and hard to walk against. The journey took even longer than before, and when the lass finally reached the moors, she had lost her way. When she finally found the right faerie mound, she put the changeling down, and sat trying to make herself comfortable. She was so tired, she fell asleep, only to be awakened by strange musical sounds. She looked in front of her and, too late, saw the faerie queen fly off, riding on her white horse. She carried a silver staff, her green velvet gown billowed all around her, and her long red hair flowed down her back, waving in the night wind. All of the little faeries floated behind her, enveloped in eerie blue light. 'Oh,' cried the lass, 'Oh, I have missed them!' What was she to do? Finally, Deirdre rose, picked up the changeling, and started on her way home. As she walked, she became more and more determined to try again. Why, she would just ask the old woman again for help. She would find out when next the faerie queen left her mound, and on that day she would be back, and this time she would not fall asleep. Thus reassured, the young lass arrived home at daybreak, fed the changeling, and headed out for the fields. It was time to harvest.

Six months passed. The entire village was perfumed by the exquisite flowers hanging off trees, growing in gardens and growing wild along the fields. Deirdre was in the market place, still holding the changeling. He was actually a darling in his own right. Such red curls, and sweet blue eyes. But his skin was pale, and growing paler. It did not look as if he would last much longer in this earthly world. He needed to be with his mother, among the faeries, just as her daughter needed to be with her.

That April morning, Deirdre happened to run into the old woman right there in the market place. The old woman, surprised to see the lass still with the changeling, asked how it had gone on Halloween. When Deridre told her her story, the old woman shook her head, 'Ah, what a shame. I'll tell you what, dearie, the fairie queen comes out again on the eve of May Day. Why don't you come to my house, spend the night and the day, and then you will be well rested? Come along then, I'll be expecting you.'

The last day of April finally arrived. The young lass, with a light and determined heart, dressed the changeling and took off for the old woman's cottage. The path was lined with magenta, purple, red-orange and white flowers, and the wind sang to her, caressed her, and helped her on her way. She was overjoyed to arrive at the old woman's home. Deirdre slept well, and the next day she rested, talking with the old woman while sipping hot tea and eating homemade biscuits. Deirdre left the old lady's cottage just before midnight. She memorized exactly where the opening of the faerie mound was, and knew just where to sit. She was wide awake at midnight, and ready for the appearance of the powerful faerie queen.

Sure enough, exactly at midnight, the faerie queen emerged from the mound, dressed elegantly in evergreen. She pointed her silvery staff and was about to give a command, when she was halted suddenly. Deirdre put her hand up to her and said, 'Stop! I have an exchange for you!'

The queen narrowed her cold blue eyes, 'Who dares to stop the queen?'

Deirdre swallowed, 'It is I!' she said, 'And I have an exchange to offer. Do you know who this belongs to?' And she held up the changeling.

The queen stared at him awhile, recognizing him as her own. 'I do,' she said, narrowing her eyes further. 'But do you know, lass, that I could turn your thoughts in such a way as to make you mad forever? Do you know that I could bring you to my faeriedom, where there is no leaving?' The young lass felt her knees buckle under, but she remembered her baby. 'Well, you see, a while ago, this beautiful changeling was exchanged for my daughter. I have taken care of him as you can see, but he won't last much longer in this world; he needs to come back to yours. And since you were the one to make the exchange in the first place, I am here to also do the same.'

'Give me that boy at once!' commanded the queen.

Deirdre felt her head spin, but she kept her voice steady. 'Not until I have my own Gwendelon in my arms!' The queen stared at Deirdre for what seemed to be an eternity. Finally, she turned toward her subjects and commanded, 'Bring the earthly black-haired girl!' Deirdre saw the faeries bounce her beautiful baby down the line. The queen at last held her, took one final look at the girl, and handed her back to the lass. Deirdre gave the changeling back to the queen.

'Well, my girl,' said the queen, 'I admire your courage. I admire the way you took care of mine, and I admire this entire exchange. I will reward you for your courage and for taking such good care of my changeling. From this day forward, you will have the courage to tell your story all over the land. And everyone in your family, for generations to come will tell this story.' The queen positioned her staff, and in moments she was off with the other faerie people flying behind, leaving a trail of eerie blue light.

Deirdre held her baby with great joy. The faeries had taken good care of her. She was plump, and pink-cheeked and was very happy to see her mother. The journey home went easily, as Deirdre cooed and spoke to her child, getting to know her all over again, which, of course, was not at all hard to do.

And it came to pass just as the queen predicted. Deirdre told her story all over the land, and her children and grandchildren and great-grandchildren passed it down. I should know as I am here to tell it to you. And may everyone have the courage to tell their own story, too.

Just as I finished the story, Karina and Jessica burst into the kitchen. They were full of their day's news, stumbling all over each other's words, each one trying to be the first to blurt out their success. Both had been chosen to be on the mediating team, no small feat, as it meant that their grades and conduct had to be near perfect. As mediators, they would be helping other, more troubled kids their age express their anger appropriately.

Arturo said something condescending, and the fighting began. I stopped them cold; there was a far more important agenda to talk about. I invited them to support Arturo and to help him find the courage to face the judge within the next two weeks. Jessica and Karina stopped their teasing and immediately began to advise their brother, at first gently, and then more forcefully.

Finally, Arturo told me he liked the story. He couldn't quite say why. I decided to let the story wash over him as I had also done with Debbie. He needed to derive his own lessons, draw his own conclusions. I did not wish to interfere with this process.

Note

1   *A Fair Exchange* from *The Maid of the North: Feminist Folk Tales From Around the World*, by Ethel Johnston Phelps (1981). Retold here by Molly Salans.

CHAPTER THREE

A Half Moon

The following week, I walked into Debbie's home, only to find no one there except her seven-year-old brother, Billy. Billy informed me that he was alone, 'but only for a second,' as he was going to go to Kelley's in 'just a minute.' Because I knew the family, and because I knew that Kelley and her sisters were just across the street, I did not believe Billy was in any immediate danger. True, it was dark outside, but then it was only 5.30 in the afternoon. However, I thought it inappropriate that he had been left alone, and I planned to report this to DSS the following morning. While Eileen might be angry with me, I knew it would also help her to think twice about leaving her children alone.

The next morning, in the office, I filed a 51A (a child abuse/neglect report) against Eileen. The intaker's voice, across the phone lines, was accusing.

'Molly, you mean you didn't call the police when you left the house?'

'No, I didn't see the need to alarm Billy in that way.'

(In general, if children are left alone, it is considered severe neglect, the police are called, and the children are removed from the home immediately. The children, who are already traumatized, but in a home they know, are traumatized twice as much through this process. At times, however, this double truamatization is necessary, in order to stop the ongoing neglect/abuse in the long run. In this case, I did not believe Billy was in any danger.)

The intaker and I continued with the report. That afternoon, my director beeped me. When I called, he asked me to come see him immediately. It was about the Carltons and the 51A.

'What happened last night?' asked Bob, once I was inside his office.

'Why?' I asked.

'Well, DSS says you were engaged in illegal activity. They actually called the district attorney's (DA) office to see if they could charge you with neglect, which in the end would strip you of your license and make it impossible for you to do social work.'

This was not making sense. Why would DSS do this?

I said, 'I can't believe this. In this situation, calling the police would have hurt the child and the family even more than they have been hurt already.'

Bob nodded: 'Well, you have worked with us for many years, and I know your work with our clients. I will handle this with DSS, but things will be sensitive for a while. I will simply tell them that we are dealing with this action on an internal level, and that we have no intention of firing you. The DA's office has not gotten back to DSS. No matter what we do on our end, as you well know, if you are convicted as charged, you will no longer be able to work with us. In the meantime, I expect you to meet with Jacklyn (my supervisor) a few times a week for a month. I will call you when I know the DA's response.'

After thanking Bob for his support, I took a deep breath on leaving the office, and canceled the rest of the day. On my way home, I fully understood how Rosa, Jasmina, Eileen, and all of their children felt. To be accused, when you are sure you are innocent, stirs up incredible shame.

That evening I called Pamela, my friend and colleague. She worked for the same agency, in a different program. She knew the DSS intaker. 'The DA is not going to convict you.' Her voice was strong and I felt her words go all the way down. 'Just let this blow over... I mean, can you imagine being a DSS worker? Have you seen the news? They are under the gun again. In the town near where we work – you know it is a different DSS office – two children were found alone, in complete and absolute filth.

'Both parents are drug addicts. The school not only has been feeding and clothing them for months, but has filed over ten 51As. Supposedly, DSS did not respond. The governor fired both the worker and her supervisor on the spot! I knew them both. I think you are caught in the crossfire. Everyone in the office is working from a state of terror. Just be still. This will blow over.'

After hanging up, I was awake most of the night, thinking about my clients. My thoughts wondered especially to Arturo. He had by now faced the judge. He either chose to speak with him or he didn't. I fully understood the depth of anxiety he must have had. He was going to have to defend himself, and he could not allow that shame to bubble forth while doing so.

How do you prove your innocence? It's one thing to have instruction, and an entirely different thing to follow through. Had I prepared Arturo fully? Over and over I reviewed our work together. He certainly had courage. He allowed me to see his shame. What could be more courageous than that? And we had gone through several role plays with him watching – and isn't watching participating? In addition, he had heard a few stories, one of which had actually helped his family and himself. Still, many doubts plagued me.

The next afternoon, exhausted and still in purgatory (as Bob still had no word from the DA), I met with Arturo. He had faced the judge, he said, and told him of his innocence. Arturo continued to tell me that the judge actually listened to him and agreed not to send him to jail. Instead, he had to meet with a probation officer once a week, and come back to court in three months. At that time, they would assess the situation. In the meantime, the judge told Arturo that he had to stay out of trouble and could not have a single criminal charge brought against him, or it would mean DYS involvement.

There was a pinpoint of silence as I digested Arturo's story. Before I could speak, Arturo thanked me for the stories I told him. I found my voice speaking from a far place, as if I were the one, this time, in need of reassurance. 'You faced the faerie queen, didn't you?' Arturo nodded, his face turning red. I noticed that the red coloring his cheeks was the red of ripe cherries warmed by the sun; it was the unexpected redness of pomegranate seed when you first open the skin, it was the kind of red which bursts forth from triumph and elation. Tears came to my eyes, and spilled like the elation spilling out of Arturo. He looked surprised. I told him I was so remarkably happy and proud of him. I asked him how he felt, talking to a judge like that.

'I don't know…scared, kind-of.'

I nodded; of course he was scared. Who wouldn't be? Even the lass was frightened, but she still stood up for herself. Arturo agreed. I commented on his courage, both in our work together and in court. We continued to talk about his triumph for a bit, then I changed the subject. I remembered that he had a failing report card. I needed to know about his grades.

Arturo shook his head, although this time he kept it high, gazing steadily at me. This change in posture was enormous. The story ingredients had sunk into his bone marrow! 'My grades are terrible,' he said, 'and my teacher says I have an attitude.'

Not surprising: I was realizing how easy it was to obtain an attitude. One had already evolved fully inside of me. It took very little for the 'Who cares?' syndrome to develop. Of course, when you are accused, you are going to have an attitude, and the last thing that will be important to you is some meaningless subjects taught in a classroom which confines your body and stifles your imagination. I understood perfectly. If you do not have a purpose, how can you possibly proceed? I told Arturo to bring his homework to the next session and to be prepared to create his own original story.

In the meantime, I was receiving nightly phone calls at home from the emergency service at work. 'Mrs Carlton would like you to call her.' When I did call her, it was to let me know how I had ruined her life by filing the 51A. She informed me that if her children were removed, it would be completely my fault. This particular evening, however, when the emergency service called, they said it was about Debbie. 'Debbie has run away. Can you give Mrs Carlton a ring?'

'Eileen? It's Molly…'

'Do you think you could get your ass up here? I have no idea where Debbie is. I am so sick of this. She never came home from the Girls' Club. Don't you see, because of that goddamn 51A you filed, all of my kids have to be in some sort of day care all of the time, night and day, unless I am home, and Debbie, as you know, fucking refuses to stay at Kelley's, and anyway, Kelley doesn't want her there because she never wants to help out, and since it's your fault and since Debbie isn't here, do you think you can come over and find her?'

It was 10pm I lived an hour away. I was a therapist, or so I thought. I didn't know at this point where the boundaries were. I wanted to swear back at Eileen. I wanted to tell her that my job was on the line due to the 51A I had filed. As this thought crossed my mind, I felt a smile cross my mouth. If only Eileen knew! We had something in common, an enemy: DSS! We were feeling the same way, that the accusations against us were false, and the only choice was to fight back. I inhaled deeply and came to my senses.

'Eileen, I am very worried about Debbie, and I know you are too. Have you called the police?'

'Called the police?! I fucking went down there an hour ago and they have done NOTHING!'

I spoke with Eileen for a good half hour, in which she calmed down and felt more at ease. I reassured her that I would come over first thing in the morning. 'We're a team, remember?' I said. 'I'm with you. Debbie should not have run. And I know how much you love her.' Eileen thus consoled, we hung up.

The therapist and family dynamics

After reporting Eileen Carlton to the Department of Social Services (DSS) and after essentially being reported by DSS myself, I, like Eileen, became unclear about where her family's boundaries were. With DSS's accusations, and the uncertainty of my position, I had allowed myself to feel like a victim. By falling into this trap, I was developing an attitude, becoming angry, resentful, and accusatory. I had difficulty speaking with Arturo because I had become like one of his sisters. When he told me of his triumphs, it was difficult for me to support him, just as his sisters find it hard to do.

In addition, Eileen was blaming *me* for Debbie's problems, in much the same way that she blamed Debbie. My immediate reaction was similar to Debbie's: I was rageful and wanted to scream back. I then wanted to *join* with Eileen against DSS. By making DSS a common enemy, blame would be averted. That was how Debbie and her mother behaved all of the time. They had been accused of so many things for such a long time that they believed they could do nothing else but blame back. It no longer mattered if the blame was justified or not. Each, unconsciously, made sure they created situations in which there could be a victim and a victimizer. And because I was feeling victimized, I became their victim!

Under such conditions, anyone would revert to harmful actions without even realizing it. In the end, writes Murray Bowen, one of the founders of systems theory, 'It is the therapist's responsibility not to get pulled into the emotional whirlpool of the family…but to be able to back up (and) achieve a reasonably broad perspective.' (Bowen and Kerr 1998, p.xii) Recognizing this helped me change my perspective on my role. I was learning to understand not only my client, but also the professionals I was working with.

That morning, when I arrived at the Carltons, Debbie had already returned home. Her mother was pacing the floor. The DSS worker was present and informed me of the following.

Debbie had left the Girls' Club at around 6pm the previous evening, with a girl eight years older than herself. They had accepted a ride from a much older man, whom neither of them knew (Debbie interjected and said her friend knew him, kind-of). They drove around town, stopping at McDonald's and the all-night Dunkin' Donuts. Debbie had walked in the door around 2am, perfectly content, as she had had a real adventure which resulted in a full meal and a yummy dessert. She was completely unaware of the danger into which she had put herself. The DSS worker left, and I glanced at Debbie. She was so young, so inexperienced. Then I looked at her mother, who was exhausted. Dark lines ran under her large brown eyes; her skin was a pasty white, and her clothing was crumpled.

I felt the trauma of their life wash over me, and I experienced very deep compassion for both of them. How could they join together as a team, to break the pattern of victimization? I began to educate them about the process of victimization, and they both sat as though spellbound. I begged Eileen not to yell at her daughters anymore, no matter how angry she became. I supported her in her anger, and gave her suggestions of appropriate punishments. I helped her carve out an hour or two so she and Debbie could spend more time together. In the middle of the meeting, Eileen stood up abruptly and said she had to go to work. She wanted Debbie in school, at least for the afternoon. Debbie agreed to go. Shortly after Eileen departed, I told Debbie the story, *A Fair Exchange.*

Her response? 'I would never let anyone take my baby,' she said. 'I would never go to work, I would always watch it… You know, my grandmother never watched us.'

Debbie ran away for attention. But she had also run because she was disclosing more and more to me about her past and she was feeling unsafe. The running acted like an antibiotic on her inner feelings of insecurity. In a perverse way, it actually had a calming effect. She needed more individual therapy to help her with these feelings of pain. Moreover, she needed to feel close to her mother in a different way. If I could have more family meetings, and bring Eileen and Debbie closer, Debbie wouldn't have to run. She would want to stay at home. She would want to help her mother, and her mother would actually relax with such changes. Could the family system handle this? The meeting that afternoon was a step. Things could change over time. Slowly. I called Eileen that afternoon and asked for another family meeting the following week. 'Debbie really misses you,' I said. 'You know how much you love her? Well that's how much she loves you…'

Just before I left the office, Bob called me into his.

'Well,' he said, 'I just spoke with Gordon Jones, the head of DSS. He said the DA can't convict you because you are not a caretaker. I told him how relieved I was, because you have worked untiringly for many years.'

I thanked him profusely for his support.

Bob shook his head. 'Just make sure you speak with Jacklyn. Don't let this happen again.'

I knew it wouldn't. I was grateful to be working in a supportive environment; how difficult Debbie's life must be without the support of her mother.

The next night, I spoke with Pamela again and briefly told her about the outcome the evening before.

Pamela told me that she had spoken with Karen, the intake worker who had accused me that very day. 'I had to call because I needed to file a 51A against one of my clients. Anyway, I got to talking with her. I didn't say much, you know, I just mentioned to her that you were one of my colleagues. She asked me what happened with everything. I told her that Bob, our director, held you in the highest regard, and that he couldn't see firing you over something like this. I told her that he had spoken with you extensively and had told Gordon the same thing I am telling you. "You know, Karen," I said, "We get a lot of support from our supervisors and directors," and do you know what Karen said? She said, "Well, you're lucky. I wish we had a director like Bob!"'

CHAPTER FOUR

A Full Moon

Emerson school is more than 100 years old, as are most of the schools in this town. Standing tall, it is solid stone, takes up three long blocks, and is directly across the street from the commons. The commons are filled with oak and maple trees and are breathlessly beautiful in April. As I stood gazing at this magnificent beauty, I wondered how children could pay attention. This park, with its luscious new grass, was bursting with life, offering fresh air and great climbing trees. It was difficult to move away from.

Inside the school, I walked down the narrow, wooden hallway, around the bend, and up the wooden stairs. I was looking for Arturo. Actually, I had seen Arturo only a few times since that moment he faced the judge. He was never home when I came, and his mother kept 'forgetting about our appointments.' Finally, I told her to call me when she needed me again, as I couldn't keep putting aside time to see him. Rosa understood and agreed.

I received a frantic call from her. 'Arturo's teacher keeps calling me. Arturo has no respect and his report cards have been awful. I told him I would call you if he didn't get better, and he didn't, so I'm calling you.' I thought, is it right to use therapy as a threat? But I didn't say anything. Looking at the need beneath this statement was what counted. At least Rosa was following through. Arturo had worse ways of screaming for help; failing grades wasn't going to put him behind bars.

'Does he go to school?'

'Of course he does. I'd bust his ass if he didn't.'

'How about if I see him in school next week?'

'That's great. Tell him he has to respect his teacher, he can't get no place without it.'

I found Arturo's class on the third floor. When he saw me standing in the doorway, he blushed and put his head down. He wasn't expecting me.

I introduced myself to his teacher, a small, dark-haired, pretty woman who greeted me kindly. She took me aside, out of the room, keeping an eye on her class while she spoke. She was one of those teachers who could sense who was out of their chairs before it happened. Constantly, without so much as glancing, she'd call out names, asking students to stay in their seats, put a zipper to their mouths, or to stop throwing spit balls. She caught each child in her accusation and was uncanny in her knowing, all the while describing in a kind, weary tone the problems she was having with Arturo.

'I tell him daily to come for after-school help. I have given him numerous ways to help him remember to bring back his homework, but I am sure he is not doing it. In school, he receives help for reading and math, but truly, his attitude is standing in his way. He is a dear boy. I can see it beneath that attitude! I am happy you are in his life.' We stepped back into the room, and she nodded to poor Arturo, who had not raised his head since I entered.

He sauntered out of the room. Obviously, I was an unpleasant surprise. Refusing to answer my questions, he walked with me into the library. The librarian led us around the school, as we searched for 20 minutes to find a room where we could have some privacy. As we searched, I wondered, had Arturo forgotten already the triumph he had experienced just months earlier? Finally settled in a small room, off the third-floor teacher's bathroom, I looked at Arturo and once again asked him how he was. He shrugged. I reminded him of his past success, and he shrugged again.

'Do you have any idea why I'm here?' He shook his shoulders.

I told him that his mother was worried about him. He agreed he was failing and had an attitude, but offered nothing else. I said to him, 'Okay, today you are going to tell me a story.'

'ME??? But I don't know any stories. I can't, I don't know how.'

I held onto this sudden burst of familiar energy. It was the same energy that had come through during that family meeting so long ago, and the same that he'd expressed when he told me of how he faced the judge. I told him that he knew millions of stories, and he just needed help to bring them forth. I pulled out some paper and a pen and began to talk. 'Look, I'll write down your every word. All you have to do is tell me the story. Now, who is going to be the good guy?' With surprising ease, Arturo told me the following story.

Figure 3. 'The Lion and the Wand' by Arturo Rodriguez

The Lion and the Wand

by Arturo Rodriguez

In 1986, in the forest, inside a cave, lived a lion. People treated the lion well. He never scared anyone. He was friendly because no one ever hurt him. He never looked mean. There was nothing special about this lion, except he had a magic wand. This magic wand could turn people and things into different people and things.

There was a young woman who lived next to the forest. She always brought the lion food. They were both friends. The lion decided to give this woman his magic wand. On that day, the lion taught her how to use it. While he was teaching her, a young man walking in the forest saw what the magic wand could do, and he wanted it. At the moment the lion gave his friend the wand, the young man decided to take the wand from the woman's hands. When he tried to do this, the lion jumped on top of him. The man got up and ran.

The lion walked the woman to her house and slept outside in her home that night to protect her. The young man did not give up.

Figure 4. 'The Lion and the Wand' by Arturo Rodriguez

He went to the woman's house the next morning. The lion already left, and the woman was still sleeping. The young man climbed through a window, and he saw the wand on a table near the bed where she was sleeping.

He went to grab the wand, and the woman woke up. When she woke up, she saw the young man running out of the room with the magic wand. Then the lion came back. He jumped through the same window and ran after the thief. He jumped on top of the man. Then he took the wand. He gave the wand back to the lady. The young man started running out the door, but the lion jumped on him again and ate him. The lion and the lady lived happily ever after.

He jumped on top of the man and took the wand. He then turned the young man into a rat. And this is why, to this day, rats are never welcome in anybody's home.

The moral of the story is: You should never take what isn't yours.

Like Debbie, Arturo really didn't want to talk much about the story after the telling. However, this tale taught me that he was struggling hard to protect his own 'magic' from thieves, from people outside of himself who, he perceived, were preventing him from succeeding, and from that part within himself that didn't believe he could succeed. It also showed me that he, unconsciously, was aware that there was something worth protecting – both the feminine aspects within himself, and the hope or magic which comes forth from such protection. His ending was positive and satisfying, as the bad guy received a just punishment. I asked Arturo to find that lion within himself, the one who could protect, the one who knew what was worthy of protection and why.

While I spoke, Arturo drew a picture to the story. He drew with unexpected enthusiasm, and had renewed energy by the end of the session. I told him I would bring the typed version back to him next week, and that he was to bring his homework to the next session. I also told him to work on his attitude. His response? 'No…No, I'll type it up. Here, let me copy it…and then I can type it!'

The spring breeze hit my face gently as I emerged from Emerson elementary school. The afternoon was wearing on, and school would soon be out. Debbie and Arturo had both introduced lions into their stories as heroes. The lion was the king of the forest, the leader, the most protective, and the most ferocious of all the animals. Debbie and Arturo both knew unconsciously that such a power exists within. I climbed into my car and pointed it in the direction of Debbie's house. I took a deep breath. I was headed for another family meeting. During the winter months I met Debbie often at school. Throughout each session, we talked about choice, the definitions of victim, and victimizer, and her role in the family. During this time I read her another story, a true tale, written in the book called *Hasidic Tales of the Holocaust* by Yaffa Eliach (1982). Before I told her the following story, *A Girl Called Estherke*, I talked about World War Two, Hitler, and the massacre of six million Jews. Debbie had not yet heard about all of this, and was amazed to learn that something this terrible could be true.

A Girl Called Estherke[1]
from Hasidic Tales of the Holocaust

In the early 1940s, Ida and her family, living in Czechoslovakia, were forced onto trains with thousands of other Jews, taking them to concentration camps. Ida's father was a very religious man, often relying on Biblical stories for guidance. On the train, he was remembering the story of Abraham and how he almost killed his son, as it was God's command. At the last minute, God stayed his hand, preventing the death. Ida's father continued to say that this war was at the hands of men, not at God's, that no one was living the commandment, 'Thou shalt not kill.' 'This is a war made by man, and must be stopped by man,' he advised Ida. 'Therefore, offer acts of kindness and acts of humanity in this inhuman time. For as the Hasidic saying goes, "If you can save the life of one person, why, it is as though you are saving the life of an entire universe."

Shortly after the train reached its destination, Ida was separated from her beloved parents. She and her older sister were thrown into a filthy room with 34 other girls. There were only three beds, which meant 12 girls had to sleep together in one cot. The filth and disease was bad enough, but the way each child was treated was worse. One morning, shortly after Ida arrived, a soldier came up to her and kicked her in the face with his boot. She watched as her pearly white teeth fell onto the floor. 'Better to have those beautiful teeth on the floor than in a pig-Jew's face.' He laughed and walked away.

One night, as the girls were sleeping, there was a terrible noise under one of the barracks. Everyone was afraid it was a family of rats. Ida was chosen to check out the situation. She reluctantly climbed out of bed, braced herself for the worst, and to her immense surprise found a much younger girl hiding. Her name was Estherke. She had long blonde curls, blue eyes and a huge dimple on each side of her mouth… She had managed to escape death by a thread, found her way into these barracks, and had crawled terrified underneath the cots. The female guard, upon learning about Estherke, told Ida and the girls that she had to be turned over to the authorities immediately. A few hours later, Ida pulled the guard over. 'Look,' Ida said, 'I know you have a boyfriend, and I know he is a Jew. Everyone in this barrack knows this, as well as many authorities outside. If you keep

our secret about Estherke, we will keep yours.' The guard immediately complied.

Estherke became Ida's joy. She lived to protect her. She saved her
her own meager bread servings, and shared them with her. Twice,
during encampment, Ida and all of those in her barracks were transferred to different camps. During each transfer, Ida managed to save
Estherke and bring her with her. Both times, Ida arranged to put
Estherke in a backpack, and in this way managed to bring her with
her to each camp she was transferred to. During the first transfer,
Ida and her sister were separated. During the second transfer, while
Ida was cleaning the bathrooms, she saw a filthy woman approaching
her and calling her name. As the woman neared, Ida could see that
her face and hair were eaten with lice and that her thin body was
starving, filthy and full of disease. When the woman was very close,
Ida barely recognized her as her very own sister! Estherke and Ida
were delighted with the reunion. But such was the sister's condition,
that when Ida was at work, her sister was thrown into the body of
corpses and carted to the corpse pile. Estherke, enraged and torn
with despair, followed the trail to the corpse pile. Among the stench
and the dead, Estherke found the older sister, and attempted to pull
her from the pile.

Ida had developed the habit of guarding her one cup of brown
hot water called coffee, and saving her portion of bread. Each night,
she shared this ration with Estherke. When she returned that
evening and heard that both her beloved Estherke and her sister
were on the corpse pile, she panicked; yet she did not give up. This
was not part of Ida's way of thinking, giving up. Ida, late that evening,
went to the corpse pile, ration in hand. She managed to find both
Estherke and her sister. She pulled them both off the corpse pile, and
little by little with luke-warm coffee, resuscitation, massage and
prayer, she managed to revive her sister. The three of them made it
back to camp that same night.

On April 15, 1945, the camp was liberated and the three
heroines made it back to Czechoslovakia. They all wished to find
family. The three agreed to separate and to meet again two weeks
later. But in two weeks, while Ida and her sister met, Estherke did not
appear. Ida was beside herself, and searched intensively all over
Czechoslovakia, and then Poland, for her. Her efforts were in vain,

and eventually she gave up. In the meantime, Ida's sister fell in love and married a man, a survivor of the Holocaust. They decided to emigrate to Israel, to spend their days in their beloved promised land. Ida was fortunate as well. She, too, married a Holocaust survivor, and they decided to create a new home in the United States.

In the early 1950s, Ida decided to visit her sister in Israel. One day, while walking down the streets of Jerusalem, she fainted right there on the street. Her body could not handle the heat. Two Israeli soldiers saw her fall, and were responsible for bringing her to the hospital. During her stay there, the two soldiers visited her daily. Their good humor cheered her and she soon became well. She asked the soldiers how she could repay them for their kindness. The older one, Yossi, said, 'I am getting married in a few days. It would be a great honor if you came to my wedding.' 'But I don't know anyone!' Ida replied. 'You know me,' said Yossi, 'and I am a pretty important member of the wedding!' A few days later Ida went to the wedding. As the music played, and the bride began walking down the aisle, Ida recognized her as her own lost Estherke! In that moment, Ida felt a strange energy enter the room. She could have sworn she felt her father's presence. She could have sworn she heard his voice whispering lovingly to her, 'Why, if you save the life of one person, it is as though you have saved an entire universe.'

The silence after this story was deafening. I wondered if it was too intense for Debbie, if the issues of abuse and neglect were too close for comfort, even in story form.

Debbie said nothing, nor did she respond to questions. I stated the story was intense, and I told her I loved the story, for the compassion and possibility it held. I told her, 'You know, Debbie, I believe you have compassion too …the way you save the cats, the way you want to help everyone. It's just that in order to really help, you have to stop hurting yourself. Each time you yell back or try to jump out a window, you hurt yourself, and if you hurt yourself, you can't help anyone. Had Ida given up, had she tried to hurt herself because her situation was so awful, she never would have been able to do the things she did. For myself, I think of Ida, and I try to find her qualities inside of me. I bet you can do the same.' Debbie looked up at me, her brown eyes shiny. 'I won't hurt myself anymore,' she said.

From that moment on, our sessions were filled with conversation about the ideas of choice, personal responsibility, when to help oneself, when to help others. Debbie's grades were improving rapidly (she proudly showed me completed homework assignments), and she was spending less time in her room at home. She gained more positive attention from Kelley, and was invited back into her house. She no longer needed to go to the Girls' Club. During these sessions, Debbie had actually stated that when her sister screamed at her, she said nothing. And when Kelley asked her to do things, she did. Instead of arguing, she was now asking questions, clarifying the directions. The major difference for Debbie, however, was that Eileen was attempting to spend one hour every few weeks alone with her. 'Mom took me to Dunkin' Donuts Saturday morning, just me! And she bought me whatever I wanted! It's good she's working... or she wouldn't be able to buy me two doughnuts!' Ironically, her second to oldest sibling, the quiet one, had now run away, and was the 'victim' in the family. Debbie was also concerned for her, but happy to be the apple of her mother's eye.

On the power of belief systems

How were the changes in Debbie and Eileen's life possible? Exactly what was causing these changes to occur? Debbie and Eileen were so similar in their needs and in the way they expressed these needs. They were both tied unconsciously to the same familial belief, which also became their personal belief. They both believed that argument and anger were the best means of receiving attention. They both thought that running away, self-humiliation, and self-mutilation, were appropriate ways of expressing inner unhappiness. Through the creation of story, however, they had a chance to re-create their personal beliefs. For Debbie and Eileen, the seeds for a new family and personal belief had been sown.

Both Eileen and Debbie desired 'lionship' – to be heard as important, ferocious, and protective. They were both looking to be protected by the other, and paradoxically, they each also wanted to be the protectors. A new thread of lioness love was beginning to weave itself through Eileen toward Debbie as, simultaneously, a new thread of self-confidence was beginning to unwind inside Debbie. Both mother and daughter had such thick defenses against their new vulnerability, so the stories acted as safeguards against too much defense falling away too quickly. At the same time, the stories were providing impetus for new thought, which in turn led to new action. Slowly, slowly, as Debbie improved her grades, as Eileen spent more one-on-one time with her, the new actions were received with praise, thus strengthening them. Each one was able to experience the other in a more positive light, so that the power of choice became more vibrant, more meaningful.

On one of my visits to Debbie's, I entered the immaculate home, and to my surprise, found both Debbie and Eileen waiting for me. Eileen greeted me, and we all walked into the living room. Debbie sat on one of the couches, Eileen remained standing. I sat opposite Debbie. Eileen began talking in a flat tone of voice, the tone she used when things were going well, 'Debbie got another good report from her teacher and she is listening to me better.'

I looked at Debbie, who was beaming on the couch. 'Eileen,' I said, 'tell Debbie you are proud of her.' She looked at me, and then she looked down. I repeated the instruction. Suddenly, Eileen blushed, her pasty white skin all red and glowing. She was still standing, but it was as if her head had shrunk into her shoulders, and suddenly she looked as if she were five years old. She seemed exposed, her vulnerable skin without defense, much like a snail without his shell. The silence grew and built. Finally, inaudibly, she said, 'Debbie, you did good.' Then Eileen turned toward a rickety old dresser. She pulled open the top drawer, and pulled out an old faded and torn manila envelope. She brought the envelope, overflowing with old photographs, and sat down next to Debbie. She spent a moment sorting through the pictures, and then spoke. 'You see this picture, Debbie? Well that's you when I brought you home from the hospital. And you see this one? That's you and your older sister... You were only two...that was when...' As she spoke, her voice grew soft, and Debbie snuggled closer and closer. Through Eileen's narrative, we were all inducted into the past – a past which Debbie had never heard about. A past filled with love, as reflected in Eileen's tone. For an entire hour, I sat and listened to Eileen tell Debbie the story of her life through photographs.

As I quietly removed myself from the room, Eileen's voice still droning into the late afternoon light, I realized I had just watched Eileen save the life of her daughter. It was as if I had witnessed the saving of an entire universe.

The flight up to Jasmina's third-floor apartment was long, the stairs narrow and winding. They were cluttered with dirt, empty soda and beer cans, stray cat urine, and food wrappers of all colors and kinds. The stench rose like heat. As I entered her apartment, I heard the usual fighting.

'Look, Molly is here. Now get your ass on the couch and listen to her.'

Andy fell quiet. He walked me to the couch and said, 'I'm hungry, I want a snack.'

'You'll eat when Molly leaves, and that's enough.' shouted Jasmina from the kitchen, which was simply the next room over.

Andy looked up at me, his round brown eyes searching mine. I wanted to side with him, I wanted to yell at Jasmina for being so unbelievably mean, but I didn't know what it was like to live in this family. I only witnessed slices of it. I had no idea what transpired daily, hourly, second-by-second. I could only imagine Jasmina's exhaustion, her parenting knowledge based on how she was parented. Jasmina, the only child of eight who was ever put in foster care and punished for her stepfather's abusive behavior – or so she saw it. For years and years, she blamed herself for her stepfather's and paternal grandfather's abusive acts toward her. She must have done something inexplicably, unforgivably terrible, or why else would such terrible things happen to her? Why else would she be the only child of eight to be sent to foster care and for what? For telling the truth to some 'damn social worker' while her mother remained in touch with, and eventually took back, the very man who abused her child?

These events informed her life and unconsciously shaped her story. They told her how to parent. Like most people, personal beliefs include the cultural story, but are also at odds with it. Jasmina believed, for example, that children should listen and obey their parents, but her own informed experiences contradicted this. The abuse she suffered informed her that adults could not be trusted, were cruel and to be feared. Because her personal story conflicted dramatically with the culture's story, and because she was completely unaware of this conflict, she could not see how her own past had a impact on her present behavior as a mother. Andy was continuously responding to her emotional reaction rather than her words.

I looked back into Andy's searching eyes. I asked, 'Do you want to write another story?' Without more ado, he wrote the following story.

Figure 5. 'The Girl and the Snack' by Andy Berto

The Girl and the Snack

by Andy Berto

A little girl is in heaven. She has no snack. She is so sad because she doesn't have a snack, and she is so sad, which is why she went to God's house. God is going to give her a cookie, and she is going to dip the cookie in the clouds, and it will come as cream.

A little girl is at home. She has no snack. She is so sad because she doesn't have a snack, and she is so sad, which is why she asked her older sister to share hers. She knew her sister would share. Not only that, but her sister knew where the whipped cream was kept. Her sister would show her how to dip her cookie into whipped cream, and the whole snack would become more delicious.

The end.

As Andy drew the picture to his story, I told him my version of the story. The atmosphere had changed. We were both more relaxed. He stated that he liked my version better, because then 'everyone shared at home.' He looked up from his drawing, his eyes searching mine again. 'God shares everything, right?' he suddenly asked, 'That's why the girl went to heaven, because she knew that.'

'Maybe you don't have to go to heaven to share,' I added. Andy gave me his beautiful smile, fell quiet, and continued to draw.

At that moment Jasmina interrupted us. 'I need to talk to you,' she said, looking at me. 'Get out of here, Andy, GO! GO DO YOUR HOMEWORK, NOW!!!' Andy jumped. I told him we could finish drawing next week. He left and Jasmina sat down. I was about to launch into another lecture about the way she treated her oldest son, but she blurted out, 'I'm pregnant…it's good news. But of course I won't continue school…' Noticing my opened mouth, she took advantage of the silence, and continued. 'Yeah, yeah, it is with Fuckhead (the children's father). Yeah, it's his kid…and no, we're not getting back together… All of the kids know, and they're excited. I'm about four months along, and it's going to be a girl… There's something else … I think I'm in love for the first time in my life. Her name is Anna.' Jasmina was beaming. 'She wants to move in, and I am fucking confused, do you think we could talk?'

I made an appointment to see her, just her, the following day.

Paradigm shift

Jasmina, just like Rosa, was doing anything she could to interrupt her own life to make sure she had no academic or financial achievement. She had been receiving straight As at school, and in the dead of winter, she had decided to have another baby with a man she despised, and soon after discovered the roots of her own sexual preference. What was I witnessing? Was this complete and absolute chaos, rising out of abusive neighborhoods, cultures, and personal experience? Or, mixed in with all of this dark history, had courage risen along with abounding generosity? Was Jasmina a complete coward, refusing to face her achievements, or was she one of the most courageous people I had ever met? To announce a preference that goes against all cultural norms, both familial and societal, had to be a brave and noble gesture. Once again, in spite of everything, I had to have respect for this family. Andy was right, God shares everything.

Two weeks later, I was sitting with Arturo. Once again, I met him at school, and we were in the same little room off the teachers' bathroom, with its windowless stone walls and wide wooden floors. Arturo brought his homework. The homework assignment was about dreams. He had a piece of paper with eight squares drawn. He was to write down a dream and draw its symbol within each square.

'I don't have any dreams,' he said, and shrugged his shoulders.

'Let's write another story,' I advised. As with our previous story writing session, Arturo's eyes shone. I coaxed him along and soon he told me the following.

Luis, Hector, and the Magic Coin

by Arturo Rodriguez

In New York, in 1988, there was a little man named Luis who had a coin that was magic. He lived in a cave in New York. He was nice, and he only went out at night. He was afraid somebody would hit him, because he thought nobody liked him. He was the size of two fingers.

After a while, there was a boy named Hector who was playing around his cave. The little man saw Hector and thought he was nice. Luis went up to the boy and started talking to him. He took his magic coin to help Hector be his friend.

Soon he gave Hector the coin because he trusted him. Hector used the coin to help him at school. He was having trouble with homework and understanding every subject. The coin helped Hector understand all of his school work.

After school, he was walking home and there was a man that saw him using the coin. The man, whose name was Angel, wanted the coin.

The next day, Hector was walking to the cave. Angel tried to take the coin away. He tried to grab the coin out of Hector's hands, but he couldn't, because Hector was holding the coin tightly.

He ran into the cave and gave the coin to Luis. Luis grabbed the coin and wished that the man, Angel, would disappear, and he did.

The moral is: Never take anything when you don't know what it is.

He grabbed the coin out of his hands and ran as fast as he could through the forest. Hector tried to run after him but found he could not keep up. He went back to the cave where Luis was waiting for him. 'Now what will we do?' asked Hector sadly. 'I will fail all my homework again... and you...' 'Not so,' said Luis. 'I don't need that coin anymore, all I wanted was a friend, and now I have you. The coin can't make us stay friends, but we have... and I can help you with your homework. You really don't need that coin to help you.'

And it came to pass as Luis said. Hector helped Luis with all kinds of things, and Luis helped Hector have courage to do his school work and to ask for help when he didn't understand. He never failed his homework again. And what happened to Angel? Well, Angel being careless, wished he would die if he ever lost that coin, and no sooner had he wished this, than he tripped over a tree stump, and the coin fell out of his hand and dropped into the nearby river. Angel's wish came true, and he died. This is why to this day people throw pennies and other coins into fountains: to remind themselves to be very careful of what they wish for, and to help Angel feel at peace.

The moral is: Friendship itself is magical, and be careful of what you wish for, it just might come true!

Arturo was amazingly verbal after telling me this story. He drew his homework himself, and began to fill in all of the eight squares with eight of his dreams! We spoke as he drew, and he told me that Hector, in his story, reminded him of himself, because he hated to do homework. However, he said, contradicting himself, 'I don't hate it right now because it's easy.'

'What do you mean?'

'I don't know. It's like that story is like a magic coin, and I wish I had a magic coin so I could do all my homework easily, and look, here is my symbol of the magic coin. But it's like I have the magic coin which is the story…' And Arturo completed his entire homework assignment with no problem.

I thought about his story, *Luis, Hector, and the Magic Coin.* Arturo was struggling with that tiny figure that could help him succeed, along with the meaner, greedier aspect of himself he called Angel. He learned that day that he could do his homework, that success occurs in increments and can happen with the magic of creativity, of story, of focus. Arturo and I met a few more times, but his mother picked up and moved to Maine. It would be two years before I would see him again.

Note

1   *A Girl Called Estherke* from *Hasidic Tales of the Holocaust* by Yaffa Eliach is reproduced by permission of Miriam Altschuler Literary Agency, on behalf of Yaffa Eliach. Copyright © 1982 Yaffa Eliach.

CHAPTER FIVE

Venus

I was sitting in Jasmina's kitchen in her new home. Six months earlier she had received notice that low-income housing was available for her. 'A fucking miracle we ever got housing, period,' Jasmina had reported to me when the house finally came through. Jasmina's partner, Anna, kept the home absolutely sparkling, and Jasmina on her toes.

Jasmina was actually more supportive of Andy as well, and this new support helped Andy stabilize his own behavior more and more.

Andy adored his new baby sister. However, it was disconcerting to watch him parent her. Jasmina not only encouraged, but expected him to do this, and she relinquished more responsibility to him. On the positive side, I wondered if the baby's complete adoration of her brother was more responsible for Andy's incremental improvements than his mother's new form of tolerance. For Jasmina continued to yell direction after direction at him, although along with this yelling came rare praise.

On this particular afternoon, Andy and I were at the kitchen table and the baby was very close. Andy described a scene that had occurred two nights before, when his father entered the home in a rage. 'He came in and started fighting with Mom, and then all of a sudden he tried to throw this table (pointing to the 30 by 60 inch table at which we were sitting) and dishes went falling and crashing, and the baby almost got hit, and Mom just started yelling and swearing. She told me to grab the baby, and then we all ran out of the kitchen.' Andy went on to describe how the fighting eventually stopped with Jasmina threatening to call the police. His father calmed down, and then they started fighting about him. His father was blaming Jasmina, telling her she was doing a lousy job with all of the children, but especially with Andy, and that she was setting a horrible example by inviting Anna (who, Andy explained, was 'really nice, nicer than Dad, and

Mom was happy') into the home. Andy told me he felt scared listening to them fight, and that everything was his fault. His head was down as he was talking, and while validating these feelings, I also reminded him of the stories we had told each other. We talked about finding the old man and the old lady inside himself, finding that self-sense of friendship. As we were speaking again, I felt the enormity of Andy's task. What role models did he have to internalize such a friendship? How did he process these sudden angry outbursts from both of his parents? Becoming angry himself only brought on more anger toward him from his mother. And yet what other choice did he have?

About anger

Anger is a normal feeling, and each person needs to know how to express this anger appropriately in each situation that arises. Accepting anger as a part of yourself, speaking directly to the person with whom you are angry, and working things through without violence, is the desired way to approach such a powerful emotion. Every child understands that the world is dangerous, that violence exists. It is our job as adults, educators, and parents not only to protect our children from this violence, but to help them build a *relationship* to the violence as well. It is a natural and normal tendency to want to protect our children from harm, and inadvertently, we deny its existence by avoiding and/or pretending it does not exist. True protection involves discussion, role modeling, and the allowance for anger, both within ourselves as adults and within our children. In this way, we can guide our children through their own feelings. Without this process, it is almost impossible to teach a healthy relationship to anger, which does lead to violence, if unchecked. If the role modeling only involves the acting out of anger, then you will raise children with the same behavior.

Thinking about this struggle, I told Andy the story of Estherke. After hearing it, he decided to tell the following story.

Mommy and the Old Man

By Andy Berto

One day, Mommy went to buy a pizza with an old man. They brought pizza home to six children.

Another day, a devil came to town. He was ugly. He had red eyes and red skin. He was sooooooooo ugly and spooky. He scared the children. He turned into a real ugly monster that had 33 eyes. He turned into the eyes. He turned one of the children into a monster, and everyone screamed. The children were so scared, they ran into their room. The monsters went after the kids. The kids were running so fast outside, but the monsters were catching up.

And then the mom and the old man were trying to kill the monsters with a knife. The devil died and the child turned back to normal.

And then the mom and the old man were trying to kill the monsters with a knife. They turned back into one devil, and the devil went running, but not before the child turned back to normal. This child used to get into a lot of trouble at home. But since he had been a monster, he became very wise. For not only did he understand the darkness of a monster by being one, but he also understood that his mother and the old man loved him enough to save him. This understanding allowed him to be the kindest and bravest child anyone had ever known.

'I wish Mom and Dad didn't fight. I wish Dad hadn't tried to hurt the baby.' Andy talked and talked after the telling of this story. We looked at the various monsters in his life, all of the violence around him, and with whom he felt safe. 'I feel safe with Mom and Anna,' he said, his clear brown eyes looking straight into mine.

Week after week, Andy began to improve by increments. He was receiving less daily 'bad behavior' reports from his teacher, and he was arguing less with his mother. With each improvement, he received more praise from his mother. As for Jasmina, she was in love, was receiving regular psychotherapy from me, and was overjoyed with her baby.

I continued to work with Jasmina off and on for another two years. One afternoon, as I was sitting with her, Arturo burst in on us, opening and slamming the back door. He was out of breath and very excited.

Arturo was always close to Jasmina, and he reported to her all of his mishaps and successes before he told anyone else. His intent now was to let her know his latest success. He had no idea I would be there, and his elation increased when we greeted each other for the first time in such a long while.

'Guess what?' he said, throwing his backpack on the floor. Head bent, he was searching for something within. Books and papers went flying, until he finally found what he was looking for.

'Look, look, I got an A… It's a story I wrote Molly, and I even drew the pictures. I remember all the stories you told me, and I love to write them now!'

I kept asking myself with amazement, over and over, what is this process called storytelling? Just how deep is its impact and power, and just how long does this impact last?

PART TWO

Anthony and the Magic Cake

CHAPTER SIX

Shooting Stars

The Gonzales family lived in a complex. The stone pathway to their home was covered with weeds, empty Dunkin' Donut bags, and coffee cups. I lifted the metal knocker on their door and let it fall several times. I also rang the bell.

Clara Gonzales opened the door, her hair was dripping wet, and a blue robe wrapped around her. It was 5pm in the afternoon, and her son, Ricardo, aged seven, and her daughter, Tanya, aged five, were clinging to her hands and waist. 'I'm sorry I'm dressed like this. It's too hot you know – I take a million showers a day. Don't mind me, come in. Were you standing there a long time?'

The children followed us into the living area. The large-screen TV took up the entire room. The room smelled of Lemon Pledge and Windex. In the center of the room was a long glass table covered with all kinds of glass and porcelain objects. Each one of them was sparkling, as well as the glass top on which they were sitting. The children knew the room well, and its rules, and managed to wiggle and move without coming near the large table. We all sat down, and Clara immediately began to talk about her son as if he weren't in the room. She flipped her head back often, slinging her blonde-brown hair behind and all around her.

'Well, you see, Ricardo has just come home from foster care. He was there because he told DSS a lie, that his father had hit him. That never happened. Ricardo has always been terrible, I mean not terrible, but argues all the time, you know? And you know, over here, DSS thinks they can tell us what to do. You know in my culture, we spank our children, that's how it is. But when my husband spanked Ricardo, which you know is different than hitting, Ricardo told DSS, and so he went into foster care.'

Ricardo was now buzzing around the room. He was jumping up trying to hit the ceiling and teasing his sister, who was now crying. She looked up at me, tears streaming down her face. She said, 'He's mean, but only sometimes. He's in my class at school.'

'That's right. You see my daughter is always honest, and he needed to stay back a grade, and I asked the school to put him and his sister together. You know, over here, nobody cares about family, but in the Dominican we care, and sisters and brothers are in the same class, if they can be. The teacher didn't like it, but I wanted him there so that Tanya could tell me what he was doing – so he couldn't lie, you know. Boy, I had to fight hard to put them in the same class, but that's what you have to do when you are a mother.'

Ricardo picked up a cushion. I walked over to him, and put my hand up to stop the throw. I couldn't imagine what a flying cushion would do to those glass objects on the table.

'Ricardo...' I said, attempting to get his attention. But he dodged me and ran out of the room.

'See, that's what he does, all of the time. He is just impossible – he never listens, although he promised if he could come back home, he would listen. But instead of helping him, DSS made my husband go to parenting class. He knows how to be a father. It's just Ricardo. I don't know what to do.'

Clara's large, deep, green-brown eyes looked sunken in their sockets. Her shoulders slumped, and she leaned back on the couch exhausted.

What was behind this scapegoating? Why was it occurring in this family? What suffering did Clara endure as a child? What hurdles were put in her way? Why was she so involved in a 'power and control' battle with her son? What or who was her son reminding her of in her own life? What was her husband's history?

As I thought about this, I pulled my crayons and paper out of my bag and asked both Tanya and Ricardo if they would like to draw. Ricardo took a flying leap across the room, almost cutting his knee on the table. As the children drew, I offered to tell them a story. Everyone, including Mom, agreed to listen. I told them an old Italian folk tale, *Anthony and the Magic Cake.*

Anthony and the Magic Cake[1]
An Italian Tale

Once upon a time, a long time ago, in a small Italian village, lived a young man named Anthony. Anthony lived with his wife and young son, and he ran a shop right in the center of town. This town was so small that everyone knew each other. Everyone knew each other so well, that the oldest of them swore they were all related. Related or no, it didn't matter, because that's how close everyone was to each other. Early one morning, Anthony went into town, the way he always did, and opened his shop. And when he walked in, he saw a dead man lying right in the middle of his floor.

The man looked as if he had been murdered, and Anthony was sure he would be blamed, for he was the only one who had a key to his shop! While he knew he didn't kill anyone, he was not sure he would be believed. He decided he would run away! Anthony made some provisions for his family, and he walked right out of town. As a matter of fact, Anthony walked for an entire year! He walked until he found a village where the customs, the language, and the food were completely different to those of his own. He found work and lodging and did not ask for wages. He worked for food and shelter for many years.

One day, the old man who was his boss, approached him. 'Son,' he said kindly, 'Son, you have worked hard and faithfully for many years, and I have not asked you a single question, but I am sure you have family who miss you. Here, take your wages and go.' And the old man handed Anthony $5000! Anthony thanked the old man, packed his bags, and walked to the nearest inn. When he arrived, and was sitting at the table comfortably eating homemade stew, he asked the innkeeper, 'What is the fastest route back to my town?' The innkeeper shrugged. 'Better to ask the old wise man, your boss. He knows everything.' When Anthony finished eating, that is exactly what he did.

'Well, now,' said the old man, 'I do know the answer, but it will cost you $5000!' Anthony struggled with this. In the end he decided to give the old man back his money. After all he hadn't had any money for years, why should it matter now?

'Well, now,' said the old man, stroking his long white beard, 'the first thing is, *stay on your path*. Don't take the low road, don't take the high road, no matter what, just stick to your path. The second thing is, *mind your own business*. No matter what, do not get involved with other people's arguments, just stay to yourself. And the third thing is, *if you get so angry you want to hurt someone, just wait until the next day.*'

Just as Anthony was turning away, the old man called to him, 'By the way, son – here, take this chocolate cake with you. When you get home, celebrate! Have it with your family…and, oh, good luck to you!'

Anthony took off and had been walking for about four months, when he ran into a group of poets. How good it felt to be in company! The poets were grand! They told wonderful stories and poems, all of which made Anthony cry and laugh. 'Hey brother,' they said to Anthony, 'We're headed up this path here – we hear there is a great carnival. Come on, come on up with us!' And Anthony was about ready to go with them when he heard the old man's voice in his head: 'No matter what, *stay on your path.*' This was difficult. The poets were so grand! 'I'll tell you what,' Anthony said, 'I'm going to stop at this inn here and have some soup. When I'm done, I'll come on up and meet you.' And they parted ways. When Anthony was sitting comfortably inside the inn, the owner started talking. 'You know that carnival up yonder? Well, I've been hearing that a bunch of thieves are ruining all of the fun… Just about everyone who's been up there has been robbed…' Anthony looked up at the ceiling and silently thanked the old man.

Anthony continued on his way and walked for another four months. He came to an inn that looked jolly enough. The innkeeper was kind and showed Anthony his room. Just as Anthony was getting under the bedcovers, he heard the most beautiful woman's voice, and she was crying and wailing. 'Oh, please let me out, please. There is a trap door just outside your room. Please come and open it, for my wicked husband keeps me prisoner here. He only feeds me bread and water… Oh, please won't you let me free?' The woman cried and cried, and Anthony's heart was torn. He threw the bedcovers off, and was halfway out of bed when he heard the old man's voice in his head: 'No matter what, stick to yourself, *mind your own business.*' This was very difficult for Anthony. He tossed and turned all night and decided to have a word or two with the innkeeper in the morning. He planned to notify the sheriff of the town as well.

When the morning came, Anthony reproached the innkeeper. The innkeeper did a most surprising thing. He fell to his knees, weeping and thanking Anthony. 'Thank you so much for minding your own business. A witch put a horrible spell on my wife and me five years ago. My wife turned into a monster, and the only way I could keep my guests and ourselves safe was by locking her up. If you had opened that trap door, she would have bitten your head off! We need three guests all in a row who will not open that trap door. You are the second one. If the guest after you does not open the trap door, the spell will be broken and my wife and I will both be free. Now be on your way, and have a good journey.'

As Anthony left the inn, he once again thanked the old man for his wisdom. He continued on his journey, and in another four months he found himself back in his village! He arrived as the moon was rising and ran to his old cottage. And sure enough, through the window he could see his wife. But what was this? Why, there were musicians, and many people in his home. Everyone was dancing, drinking, and eating wonderful things. Why, there was a magnificent celebration occurring! But in the next moment, Anthony saw his wife dancing with another man...and then she kissed him! This was too much for Anthony. He put his hand into his pocket and pulled out his knife. He had always been faithful to his wife, and didn't he tell her he would return? His anger was making his entire body shake, and he could hardly contain himself. And then he heard the old man's voice in his head: '*If you get so angry that you want to hurt someone, just wait until the next day.*' Anthony struggled and fought with himself for a long time. This was his hardest task. But finally he put his knife away, turned around, and walked to the nearest inn. There, in his room, he plotted the death of his wife the whole night through. He rose with the sun the next morning and went to his old cottage. He was surprised to see the candles burning, the stove lit, and his wife already cooking. He knocked, thinking he would stab her as soon as she opened the door. Yet when she saw her beloved husband (for she recognized him immediately) she threw her arms around him. 'Anthony, oh Anthony, I cannot believe you are home! And what a day you have picked!' And as she was greeting him thus, into the kitchen walked the man she had been dancing with the night before. 'Look, look,' she cried, 'this is our son! And he is now 18, and he has been accepted into the finest school of medicine in the country! He is leaving this very morning, and I am cooking him a very special breakfast and...' This time it was Anthony's turn to fall to his knees in gratitude. He thanked the old wise man over and over. For his advice had saved the lives of the two people he loved most in the world.

Anthony suddenly jumped up and said to his wife. 'Hold on! I left something back at the inn... I'll be back in a second.' Anthony ran back to the inn, burst into his room, and picked up that chocolate cake the old man had given him one year ago. Why that cake was as fresh as the day he received it! He ran back home, and presented the cake to his wife and son. They all sat down to a scrumptious breakfast, and then Anthony took out his knife and cut the cake. As he cut that cake in half, out fell the $5000!

When I had finished telling the story, you could have heard a pin drop. 'What did you like about the story?' I asked. But there was no response. 'Well, did Anthony remind you of anyone?'

'Yes,' said Tanya, 'Ricardo...'

'Uh...uh...no...!'

'Yes, 'cause you don't listen.'

'What made Anthony listen?'

'The old man!' This from Ricardo, 'He was lucky to get $5000.'

'Was he lucky, or did he earn it?'

There was silence. There was more silence after the next few questions. I decided to allow for the silence, because I knew the story would work into their subconscious minds, and I did not wish to disturb this process. Instead, I looked at their drawings. Ricardo proved to be a gifted artist and an imaginative thinker. I praised his artistic skills, trying to model for his mother new ways of communicating with him. She readily agreed that he was a great artist, and wished out loud that Ricardo would listen to her, the way Anthony listened to the old man. Since time was running out, I asked each child to think about this story, and maybe they could write their own at the following session.

'What's your name?'

'Do you want to see what I can draw?'

'Can I draw?'

'Me too.'

Four children banged into me as Maria Vera opened the door. 'Kids, get away from here and leave the lady alone. Hi, how are you, Molly?'

I was carrying drawing paper and an opaque box filled with crayons, colorful feathers, sequins, and glue. I nodded, and the children continued to clamor.

'I said leave Molly alone…you ain't bein' polite, none of you…I SAID LEAVE HER ALONE – NOW GET TO YOUR ROOMS NOW!'

Three of the children jumped and ran, one of them made a flying leap for the couch, and jumped on it.

'JUAN, STOP NOW!' He jumped off the couch, and sat, punching the air with his fists.

'I'm sorry, now I'm not bein' very polite. Come in and sit down – how was your weekend?'

It was now Wednesday.

'You see, he's why I called you, you already see how he is. Juan just never listens, he ain't a bad kid or nothin'.'

I sat down on the same couch Juan was bouncing on. Maria sat in an armchair across from me. The TV took up much of the small living area. There was a black-painted shelf behind Maria holding many glass and porcelain objects. The brown-orange carpet was worn thin and matted with grey and white cat hair.

I took a deep breath. The apartment smelled of rice and chilies, stale cigarette smoke, cat hair and perfume. I had tried to make an appointment with Maria for the morning so that we could talk without the children present, but she hadn't had time until late this afternoon.

'See, I'm in court all day long. What with my ex bein' in prison and me havin' to go to court for nothin', and of course Juan and Gabriella miss him and the other two, Angel and Pedro, will forget their Dad, he never been around. And the other day Juan got so mad at my boyfriend that – you see that rabbit over there?' she pointed to a small glass rabbit sitting on the rickety shelf, 'Juan just picked that up and tried to throw it at him, only my brother stopped him, but then Juan was kickin' and punchin' so much he knocked the whole shelf down and my boyfriend managed to catch it. But what a mess! And then the teacher keeps on writin' notes 'bout how he ain't sittin' still or listenin' or nothin'…and I keep sayin', Juan, you have to be good…but he just don't listen…'

What a life Maria described in her flat tone of voice. She was only 24 years old with four children. Two of them did not know their father, and the other dad was in prison. What made Juan's father turn into a criminal? Was he himself acting out a family shame that went undiscussed, thereby continuing to pass down this shame to his son?

Between Maria's need to gravitate toward unhealthy relationships, and the criminal/abandoning behavior of the fathers, Juan and his siblings were experiencing a mass of unconscious, unexpressed feelings, which Juan was now acting out. Added to the complications were the expectations that were put on him. Because there was no steady male figure around, like Andy, Juan was expected to parent his younger siblings, while also remaining a child who would take orders from adults. As the oldest sons, Ricardo and Juan were both carrying the same weight of expectation. However, what was different for Ricardo was that his father was still a part of the family.

Juan was jumping off and on the couch again. 'Hey, Juan,' I said, trying to gain eye contact unsuccessfully, 'I'm getting a little seasick here – this couch is getting a bit rocky. Do you think you would like to color?'

He flew from the couch to the floor. 'Ready to color,' he said, finally looking at me and charming me with his delightful smile. I placed the material on the floor beside him.

'Would your other…'

'GABRIELLA, WE GET TO COLOR!'

Two more children came bounding in.

Gabriella walked right up to me. She gazed at me with her green-brown eyes shaped like almonds, her dirty blonde hair falling in waves down to her waist. 'May I color now too?' she asked in a whispery voice.

'Thank you for asking nice,' her mother said.

Then Maria said, 'And then the other day the police came, and I didn't do nothin'…and they talked to my brother 'cause he was here, and he said we didn't do nothin'.'

'He said you didn' do *fuckin'* nothin'.'

'JUAN!'

'Juan, were you here when the police came?' I asked.

'Yeah, and they put those cuffs on her and took her away, and the police car drove away with her in it.'

'Yeah, he was here and everythin', and the police told me they just wanted to ask me some stuff, and I said, well then, come in – no, they just put those cuffs on me and said they had some questions at the station and my brother was here to watch the kids, but Juan was awake when I come home so late, and you know I was supposed to have a job interview that day too.'

'Yeah, Mom come home real late.'

'Why were you still up so late?'

'Don't know...' Juan kept his head down. He was drawing intently as we talked. He was completely still. This was the first time this family was discussing this incident. And they were discussing it openly with a complete stranger.

'Well, that's what happens sometimes. Juan is a real light sleeper, he's like me, and when he can't sleep, well then, he's in my bed, and when that happens somehow all the others hear him leavin' the room and then all four of them are in bed with me.'

'Why were you arrested, Maria? And when did this happen again?'

'They thought I was doin' drugs or sellin' or somethin', I mean it just happened the other day.' What I was realizing about Maria was that she was not putting time in its proper sequence. To her, 'just the other day,' could mean yesterday, or six months ago. I gave up trying to figure out the time sequence. That wasn't the point, and Maria was speaking so fast and saying so much there just wasn't time to try and clarify this.

'You know, it's the neighbors across the street, they's the ones doin' drugs but I don't say nothin', I mean they ain't botherin' me, but I think it's bad for the children.'

'The police told Mom not to fight or nothin', just come nice and good.'

'Is that what you heard the police say, Juan? What did you do after Mom left?'

'Nothin'. Uncle Juan was here, but he went somewhere.'

'How did you have dinner?'

'Oh, I always leave a big pot of food on the stove and they already ate, you know, when they got home from school.'

I couldn't help but notice Juan's stillness. What made him pay attention and listen and participate here, right now, when he couldn't do this elsewhere? What was it about the telling of his own story that helped so completely with attention?

'We humans are a storytelling lot,' writes Marni Gillard. 'We drink in stories from…our games on street corners, our…moments with relatives, babysitters, neighbors and friends…we are fed stories by the world.' (Gillard 1996, p.29) And since each and every one of us is a part of the world, then we need to tell our stories back. The very participation in the telling of our own stories creates an identification, a place for our own experience which may otherwise not be there, if the story remains untold.

Juan was actually participating in the telling of his *own* story, within his *own* family. His unusual stillness and attentiveness showed the impact of being involved in this story. I asked myself several questions. What role models did Juan have? And what type of model did the police play out for Juan? Of course, they were doing their job. Yet through the eyes of a seven-year-old, what was his *experience* witnessing his mother being handcuffed and taken away by policemen? What were they teaching him about respect and authority? What had his father taught him? I looked over at Maria. Her dark brown eyes had softened as she spoke, and her short black hair looked matted around her face. Only 24 years old.

I tried to make another appointment with her alone, but failed. I agreed to come back the following week with art material in hand, and a story in mind.

Note

1 *Anthony and the Magic Cake* is a story I heard told by David Whyte many years ago. Interpreted and retold by Molly Salans.

CHAPTER SEVEN

Too Exhausted to Make a Wish

'Can I draw?'

'Molly, watch this!'

'Me too...me too.'

This was my fourth visit to Maria Vera's home.

'Come on, kids... Hi, Molly, come in. How was your weekend?' Maria asked. 'I think you should sit at the table, I set it all up for you. I think you should just meet with Juan, but if you want to meet with everyone 'cause everyone wants to color, that's okay too.'

'Well, what if they colored for a while, and you told me how they were doing?

'Well...see, I set it all up...'

'Oh...no problem. Do you want to join us for a little while? I was going to tell them another story.' I had told them the story of *Anthony and the Magic Cake* the week before. I was curious to see how they would respond to it.

'You were gonna tell another story... Well, I could start cooking a little bit for tomorrow.'

'MOLLY, SIT NEXT TO ME!' Gabriella yelled from the kitchen.

Juan had me by the hand, 'Come on, I'll show you,' he insisted, pulling me. And Angel and Pedro followed.

Right in the middle of the kitchen, Maria had set up a wooden table with two benches attached. It was the sweetest little set-up I had ever seen. The table was newly sanded and polished, and smelled of thick lacquer. It was the color of rich pine and was quite a contrast to the beige vinyl floor tile, which was worn thin and coming apart around the edges of the room. The regular kitchen table had been pushed to the side, and the new table was barely large enough to hold three people. 'How do you all sit and eat?' I asked Maria at one point. 'Oh, you know kids,' she answered, 'They're all hungry at different times. Nobody eats in here, either. You know, we sit and watch TV, or if it's summer we're outside.'

Maria explained the new table, 'I pulled it out of my neighbor's yard the other day... (about a month before) and my boyfriend and brother fixed it all up. I don't think it will break, but it's not perfect or nothin'...'

The four children and I fit perfectly on the benches, and there was just barely enough table room for everyone to draw.

Gabriella looked up at me. Her full mouth was pursed. 'Now are you going to tell us somethin' like last time?'

'Yeah, tell us a story...like magic money!' Juan shouted.

I looked at Maria. She shrugged, and said, 'I don't know if it does any good. Juan still don't listen or nothin'.'

'Uh huh... I listened to the teacher.'

'Oh, Juan, quit your lyin'. I tell you it ain't any good. A story is fine.'

I told them the story of *The Fairy Grotto*.

The Fairy Grotto[1]
A Vietnamese Tale

A long time ago, in a small village in Vietnam, lived Tu Thac, the great tax accountant. Tu Thac was sitting in his small office at his large desk. His desk had two drawers, one on either side of him. In one drawer were two small chests. Both chests held many gold coins – one chest contained Tu Thac's savings, which were substantial, and the other chest contained the taxes the people had paid over the years.

In the other drawer was Tu Thac's personal writing journal. For Tu Thac was a poet and a songwriter, and no one in the entire village knew this, not even his family. Tu Thac was happily writing, when a peasant woman burst into his office. She was dressed in shabby clothes, and she was carrying a baby in one arm and a flimsy cloth purse in the other. She threw the coin purse down on Tu Thac's desk and cried, 'Please don't take my land. I know this is only a few pennies, but it is all I have. My husband died just a few months ago and I have had to do everything myself, and what with no rain and the terrible crops, please give me a few more months to pay my taxes.'

Tu Thac looked up at her and picked up the enormous black volume. He kept it standing in such a way that she could not see what he was doing. 'Name?' he asked. She gave her name. He found the name in the volume and crossed it out. He then opened the drawer which contained all of the gold coins, opened up his chest with all of his savings, removed several gold coins, and put them in the tax box. Then he said, 'Look, here. Your husband must have taken care of everything before he died, as the property is completely paid for. Now go on with you.'

In disbelief, the peasant thanked Tu Thac and left. Tu Thac went back to his writing, but he looked up with a start. The sun was setting, and he suddenly remembered that tonight was the Spring Festival, a time when people from miles around came to celebrate the festival of flowers. And they came to this village in particular because of the rare peony tree that had blossomed suddenly right outside the courthouse a few years before. Tu Thac shut the drawers to his desk, put the volume away, put on his great overcoat, locked the office, and walked quickly toward the center of town. When he arrived, he ran into throngs of people. The area was so crowded he could hardly move. However, there was tremendous trouble somewhere near the courthouse. He heard guards yelling and people shouting. He made his way through the crowd until he reached the center of the commotion. Standing in front of the courthouse, right underneath the peony tree, was the most beautiful, most frail-looking woman he had ever seen, and she was crying. 'I didn't mean it,' she wailed, 'Honestly, I didn't mean it.' But the guards were threatening her.

'Hold on,' cried Tu Thac, 'What is happening here?'

'Do you see that peony flower, sitting there in the dust? Why this young, no-good woman thought she could steal it.'

'No, no, it wasn't like that. I had never seen such a plant, and I had to smell it. All I did was reach up to pull it down, and it simply fell off.'

'Clearly you can see this is a mistake?'

'Mistake or no,' cried the guards, 'she has ruined a peony, and for that she will be punished, and she must pay.'

'Here,' said Tu Thac, removing his magnificent overcoat, 'Accept this as payment for the broken peony and let this fair maiden take her leave.'

The guards gladly took Tu Thac's coat. They full well understood its value and let the young woman leave without further ado.

The young woman thanked Tu Thac and disappeared among the throngs of people. However, all through that night, Tu Thac could not stop thinking of this beautiful girl. Why hadn't he at least asked her for her family's name? After a sleepless night, Tu Thac decided he was going to find her.

He packed some provisions for himself, including his little black notebook, dropped his key ring at the doorstep of his parents, and headed for the mountains. He had no idea where he was going or just exactly how he was going to find the young woman. He walked for a long time, writing new songs and poems, becoming familiar with mountainous terrain, and taking in the beautiful and rare natural sites he discovered. One morning, he came to the edge of an inviting river and found a boatman. Tu Thac had been alone for a long time and he was delighted to find another human being. He asked the boatman to take him down the river, and said he would pay with songs, stories, and poems. The boatman agreed, and the two rode down the river, entertaining each other for many days. However, one morning Tu Thac was struck by a particular mountain they were drifting toward. The day was foggy, but at the base of this mountain there was a fantastic play of color created by the way the fog hit the base of the mountain, the way the sunlight, reflecting the mountain and river colors, filtered through the fog, and the way the water itself played into the dance of light and reflection. Tu Thac asked the boatman to leave him off at this place.

When Tu Thac reached the exact place of color play, he leaned against the mountain in order to have a closer look. However, when he leaned against this mountain, it actually moved! Tu Thac saw that a door to the mountain had opened! He walked into the passageway and could not believe what he saw. The ceiling, the walls, and the floor were all sparkling with the rarest of gems, stones, and crystals! As Tu Thac walked along in disbelief, two young maidens dressed in sea-blue colors greeted him.

'Welcome, Tu Thac. Come, follow us – the queen and her daughter await you.'

Tu Thac followed the young, ethereal creatures into a magnificent room, and sitting on lush magenta cushions was a stunning queen.

'Well,' said the queen graciously, 'you have finally arrived. We have been waiting! But of course you have no idea where you are! Please have a seat. You see, I am queen of the eighth fairy grotto. There are eight grottos just like this one all over the area, only they are very hard to find. It is only by the way the sun, the fog, the river, and the mountain distribute their colors that anyone ever finds us …but you have! And this must be the happiest day of your life, for this is the day of your wedding!' Just as the queen said this, in walked the lovely maiden Tu Thac had saved! She was dressed in a dazzling white gown in the shape of flower petals, and her long, blue-black hair shone like stars. Tu Thac was beside himself with joy. The wedding was lovely and the feast tremendous. And the days spent with his new wife were even grander. Each day they took a different walk, and each walk was more exquisite in natural beauty than the one before. Tu Thac and his wife had endless things to say to each other, and they enjoyed each other's company tremendously.

When they had been married for about one year, they took a walk, which happened to give them a view of the river on which Tu Thac had traveled. Suddenly he was homesick. He turned to his wife and said, 'My dearest, I have not been home for one year! My family has no idea where I am, nor do they know how happy I am. Why, I must return home just for a few days to tell them.'

His wife's eyes filled with tears. 'Our way is very different from the world you have come from, my husband, but I can see how much you wish to return. Just take this note from me and remember to read it while you are gone. Go to my mother – she will help you return.'

'My wife,' Tu Thac laughed, ' I will be gone just three days, I promise!'

The queen acted strangely as well: 'Mark my words, it is very hard to find us; it is by luck you will find the exact play of color and light between mountain, river, fog, and sun. But I see you must return.' The queen ordered a vessel for Tu Thac, and no sooner had he entered the vessel than he arrived on the shores of his hometown. Tu Thac jumped out of the vessel elated. He ran up the beach toward town. When he arrived he stopped dead in his tracks. The town had completely changed, and so had all of the people walking about. They were all dressed differently. He walked down the streets, looking for his old office. When he couldn't find it, he asked an old lady for directions to the tax accountant's office. She pointed down the road to a large stone building. 'Up the stairs, through the front door, and down the first hallway, third door on your right.' Tu Thac followed her directions, and soon came to the door marked 'Tax Accountant.' When Tu Thac knocked on the door, the accountant shouted, 'Yeah, come in.'

'Pardon me,' said Tu Thac, bowing, 'I am Tu Thac, the tax accountant.'

But the other laughed. 'That's a good way to get out of paying taxes, I haven't heard that one before!'

Tu Thac became puzzled. 'No, truly, just last year…'

'Impossible,' the other replied. 'My father was tax accountant for the past 30 years, and I took his place last year.'

'Will you help me?' asked Tu Thac, 'I am not lying. I must search the volumes to show you I am correct.'

The other agreed to help Tu Thac. They pulled down volume after volume searching for Tu Thac's signature. Finally, the current tax accountant found Tu Thac's records. 'Here you are,' he said, 'Tu Thac, tax accountant…' and then he looked up at Tu Thac with an odd expression on his face, 'But that was 300 years ago.'

In that moment, Tu Thac understood that one year of fairy time was worth 300 years of human time! He thanked the accountant, and walked back toward the beach. It was then he remembered the queen's words: 'It is only by luck anyone ever finds us.' He thought too of his wife's tearful remarks: 'Our way is very different to your way…' and then he remembered his wife's note. He reached into his pocket, pulled it out, and read: 'My dear Tu Thac, no matter what always, always remember me.'

Tu Thac quickened his pace. He had no idea if he would ever find his beloved wife again, but he knew he would spend the rest of his life trying.

'That isn't fair,' cried Maria, who stood mesmerized during the entire telling of the story. 'They should be together…but ain't that just like everything. You have sometin' and then you don't.'

No one else said anything for a while. Then Juan said, 'Mom's boyfriend hits me.'

Maria looked stunned.

Slowly, Gabriella nodded her head. 'I seen him do that,' she whispered.

'What does he hit you with?' I asked.

'A belt, and it hurts.'

'When does he hit you?'

'Sometimes when I be bad.'

'Is Mom home?'

All the children said 'no' in unison. Maria had had no idea.

I brought Juan into a bedroom in order to see if he had any bruises or marks. There were a few deep marks on the backs of his legs.

I talked with the children some more, and then I sat with Maria.

'I didn't know…' she kept shaking her head. 'But you know, Juan is so bad.'

'Maria, no one deserves to be hit. No one.'

'No, see, this is why I can't get a job or go nowhere… I didn't know.'

I let Maria know that I would have to talk with DSS. 'Maria, I don't know if you can understand me or believe me or not. You have really good children. They are excited and imaginative, and they want to please you so much. But when a grown-up acts mean, then children will copy what the grown-up does. This may be one reason why Juan is not improving… Hitting hurts children on the inside as well as on the outside.'

'My dad hit my brother all the time. I wish things could be like those stories you tell.'

'Maria, have you ever told anyone about your dad and brother?'

She shook her head.

'Have the children ever told you about your boyfriend hitting them?'

She shook her head.

'This is your story and your children's story; the truth of these stories and me hearing them and you telling them far outweighs what happens in the stories I tell you. Thank you so much for letting me know your children. I know how precious they are to you.'

Maria stared at me. Her tone remained flat as usual. 'Well, thank you, Molly. Have a good weekend.'

It was late September. Clara invited me into her immaculate living room, and she placed her infant in the infant seat sitting on the floor. Tanya and Ricardo were watching television. Clara asked Ricardo to turn off the TV several times. She screamed the direction on the fourth try. Hearing Clara scream, Ricardo's father, Jorge, walked into the living room.

He was a short, stocky man with penetrating brown eyes. 'What's going on here?'

'Nothin'.' Ricardo grumbled.

Clara wearily pushed her hair out of her face. 'Ricardo is still having trouble in school. He's been diagnosed with ADHD (attention deficit hyperactivity disorder) and he is taking Ritalin, but he just don't listen to his teacher. I tell him all the time, why don't you behave?'

'Yeah,' Tanya agreed, 'he's in trouble all of the time.'

Jorge looked at Ricardo. 'You can't be behavin' like that no more, Ricardo, you have to learn to have respect.'

Ricardo and Tanya exchanged glances, and they each left the room, one after the other, without saying a word.

'He don't have no respect, that is the problem.'

'And what happens in this home when he doesn't show respect?'

'What, you think I hit him? You think that's why he was in foster care? Know what? I wish I could hit him, my father hit me, and the Bible says, "Spare the rod and spoil the child." You see how spoiled he is? Don't listen to no one. And you guys, you and DSS, they tellin' me what to do as a father. Ricardo would change if I hit him.'

'You know hittin' ain't right,' Clara said softly.

'You trying to tell me what to do too? Trying to turn me into a girl?'

On Jorge

Jorge grew up in a community learning about the negative side of machismo, and was raised by a father who beat him. He was sensitive and aware enough to stay married to the same woman and to remain within the family unit, despite feeling 'punished' by DSS and feeling 'forced' to go to parenting classes, and despite Ricardo's diagnosis of ADHD. If he were feeling isolated before all of this, surely his sense of isolation increased during the process. Regardless of the truths or falsehoods of all that he was accused of, his 'machismo' or 'manhood' was at stake. However, Jorge courageously participated in psychotherapy and family storytelling, thereby reclaiming his place in the family and ending his sense of isolation.

It was a paradox. He was feeling isolated. The more he felt isolated, the more he isolated others, until the very acts of isolation caused him to be violent, as a means of making connection. However, this violence created more isolation and did not give him the connection he was truly looking for. The way to connect more kindly was through talking about his experiences, but this action was completely counter to his belief system, which instructed him that talking was 'girlish.' He had lost his ability to be compasionate. The very act of participating in family storytelling restored compassion to his heart.

'May I ask you something?' I asked Jorge.

'Go ahead.'

'Through hitting you, did your father teach you to respect him? Or did he teach you to fear him?'

'Both...you just didn't disrespect my father or nobody else.'

'Did you fear your father?'

'I didn' fear nothin'. Never cried when that belt came near me.'

On changing patterns

Jorge could not make the distinction between fear and respect. How could a distinction like this be made when you were being physically beaten, and when fear and respect became so inter-twined it was impossible to separate them? This entwinement of emotion not only continued to exist in Jorge, but was being passed down to his children in a continued motion of anger and inade-quacy. Ricardo's defiance was reminding Jorge of his own inade-quacies and traumatic past, and this dynamic only fueled his angry defense.

By participating in telling a story, the family might move away from giving negative attention to Ricardo. A story could also introduce a sense of mutual creativity between all family members: it could help the family become more positive by understanding that they could have fun together.

How could a pattern like this be turned into its opposite? At this point Ricardo and Tanya came back into the room. Tanya again sat next to me. Ricardo went over to play with the infant. Suddenly, he shouted, 'Hey look, the baby's laughing!' Everyone looked over at the baby who was smiling widely, right into Ricardo's face, and Ricardo was mirroring the baby's smile. Everyone started laughing. The power Ricardo had in this family became apparent. He could make everyone angry at him as easily as he could make everyone laugh with him.

I wanted to pull on the strength of this new positive pulse I was witnessing in the family. I suggested that the family tell a story together. The children jumped right in, and because of their enthu-siasm, Mom and Dad followed suit. I didn't even have a chance to ask about the previous tale, but I trusted that the story was working deeply.

'Okay,' I said, 'We're going to take turns deciding the characters, the magical object and the time and the place. Tanya – who should be the good character?'

'I don't know.' She put her head down shyly and giggled.

'Tanya, don't be like this, just answer the question.'

'I don't know how to write a story.'

'I know, Superman!' cried Ricardo.

'Let's go over this a little more. First of all, the rules: when you make up a story with me, you can't use characters you already know about – no movie, book, computerized or TV characters.'

'Oh, that's not fair! I can't do this.'

'Ricardo, just listen to the rules.'

'I'm hearing a lot of "I can'ts." Has anyone here ever tried to do this?'

'No!'

'Then how do you know if you haven't tried? Everyone knows how to write a story, it's just that you need some help. And I'm going to help you. Now a character can be anything. It can be a person of any age, or it can be any type of animal. Tanya, first thought – just blurt it out – who can be the good character?'

'Ummmm...a dragon!'

'NO! A little boy!'

Tanya's face fell as she looked at me.

'Ricardo, you will get your turn, right now, this is Tanya's turn.'

'Oh, I hate this! This isn't fair at all.'

'Tanya,' I said, turning my attention away from Ricardo. 'Good job! And that's great. Now, Ricardo, good listening this last second! You have a choice to pout or to join in, and right now it's your turn! Who is going to be the dragon's friend?'

'A baby bird. No...a giant baby bird!'

'This is wonderful! Mom, who is going to be the bad character?'

'Spiderman!'

'Ricardo, enough!' Clara was annoyed. 'You already heard the rules! No characters you already know, and now this is my turn. You have to wait your turn. You see, Molly, this goes on all day!'

'Hmmmmm...all day? Ricardo, are you like this all day?'

'NO! Come on, Mom, hurry up, who is going to be the bad guy?'

'Good job, Ricardo, for getting us back to the story!'

'Ummm... How's about a mean old lady?'

'Yes!' shouted the children.

'Okay, Dad, is there going to be a magical object?'

'Of course!'

'What do you mean?' asked Ricardo.

'Well,' chimed in Clara, 'a stone, a feather, something like that, right?'

I nodded.

Jorge shrugged his shoulders. 'Come on, Dad...' whined Ricardo.

'How's about a magic ring?' offered Tanya.

Dad agreed.

'No, I don't want it to be a magic ring, I want the dragon to have magic on him.'

'Ricardo...' warned Jorge.

'Boy, Ricardo,' I said, 'you have so much energy and imagination. All you need to do is learn to listen, just like Anthony in that story I told last week. Who wants the magic object to be a ring?'

Everyone, but Ricardo, agreed.

'A magic ring it is.'

'Oh, this just isn't fair!'

The children decided on a time and a place.

'Now, you begin to create the story. Just like this: What is the first sentence? How does it begin?'

'Once upon a time...' began Clara.

'Now, why was the dragon nice? And why were the baby giant bird and the dragon friends?'

'I know,' shouted Ricardo, 'everyone in the forest was poor, and the dragon and the bird wanted to help everybody! And then the wicked lady killed everyone. And then...'

'Hold on, Ricardo, remember this is a family project. Let everyone suggest.'

'Yeah!' said Tanya, 'and the magic ring helped them feed everybody, only a mean old lady stole the ring!'

'How did the magic ring appear? And then what happened?' I asked, writing furiously while the family created the following tale. Afterward, while they drew pictures, I added my own ending.

The Tale of the Dragon

by Ricardo, Tanya, Clara, and Jorge Gonzales

Once upon a time, a long time ago, in the forest was a dragon. He helped everybody. When he was a baby, a giant bird gave a magic ring to him to be nice to sick people and to give food to the people. The dragon and the giant, they were best friends. A mean lady lived there, too. She was rich, but she never gave anything to help. She just wanted to be rich, everything to be for her. She stole the magic ring from the dragon.

All the animals who were hungry died, and all the friends became sad. The dragon got sick. The giant bird saw his friends sick. Everyone knew the mean lady stole the ring but no one knew how to get it back. The giant bird told the dragon he had to get the ring back from the mean lady.

The bird told the dragon to fly on his back. Then they flew to the mean lady's house. The dragon knocked the door down. Even though he was sick, he could still do that. They got into the house. They looked under the bed, they looked on the sink, inside the stove. Then the dragon yawned. He saw the magic ring on the ceiling when he lifted his head. It was taped up there.

The giant bird made the dragon better with the ring. Everybody got better. Then the old lady's house crashed because the ring from her ceiling was gone. The house crashed down on the old lady, and she died.

The moral is: Look well for things and don't want everything just for you.

It is said that even today the dragon and the giant bird can still be heard in the forest. They used to love to sit by the river banks, underneath the trees. When the dragon was happy, his tail would waggle and pound so much that the very streams echoed with the strong sound. And the bird flapped his wings in excitement so often, that the winds imitated and sang the same sounds. So whenever the rivers gurgle forcefully and the winds rush loudly, everyone within the forest knows that the dragon and the giant bird are still present.

Clara was laughing by the end of the story. She said that Tanya was constantly losing things. Tanya was glowing. As they drew pictures to their story, Ricardo was completely still and attentive.

Reflections on the Gonzales family

It was dark as I walked outside and I was deep in thought as I got into my car. I had no idea what would come of this story. The family was working through deep feelings of hopelessness and hopefulness. What did each character represent for the family? Who was the mean old lady in the family dynamics? Clearly, the story represented hope, for the characters were able to conquer and kill the mean old lady, albeit accidentally.

And what was Jorge's role in this family? How left out and abandoned was he feeling? I was startled by a knock on my window. When I looked up, a gang of very tall, large young Hispanic men had surrounded my car. The man who knocked on my window was smiling, his beeper in one hand. With the other hand, he was beckoning me to open my window. My heart beating faster than death, I turned on my engine and swerved away as fast as I could. All the way home, on safe familiar roads, I turned over some huge assumptions in my mind. Were these young men abandoned by their fathers, too? And were they themselves fathers who were now abandoning their sons? Were these the external circumstances in which Ricardo and his sister were growing up?

The heroes in this story, a dragon and a bird, are both large and small. They are best friends and could possibly represent father and son. They help each other get rid of the mean old lady. In the end, the characters are able to conquer evil and restore peace and kindness to their friends.

The death of the old lady symbolizes the death of a life or a way of thinking no longer valued by Ricardo or any member of his family. When she dies, the more generous sides of life flourish. Moreover, the diseased character, the dragon, is both intrinsically good and continues to try to help, regardless of how ill he is. The development of this character points to the fact that the family system is wholeheartedly intact, and they are trying to find their way back to that wholeness. In order to do this, they have to confront the 'old lady' within their family system – that is, the force which keeps creating mean-hearted actions. The story shows that the joint effort of the ill character and his friend can conquer these kinds of mean-hearted actions by first confronting them. They not only fight the old lady face-to-face, but they also enter her place of dwelling to face this place of meanness with their true hearts. Ultimately, kindness has triumphed over meanness.

I chose to elaborate on the ending rather than change theirs, because both children, Ricardo, in particular, understood that life isn't fair, nor always kind. In particular, I wanted to show, through my ending, that honesty, peace, and kindness are a result of confronting the meaner aspects of yourself. The very energy it takes to create tragedy is the same energy it takes to create kindness and honesty.

Note

1 *The Fairy Grotto* from *The Brocaded Slipper and Other Vietnamese Tales,* by Lynette Dyer Vuong (1982). Retold here by Molly Salans.

CHAPTER EIGHT

Light Years Away

It was an icy January morning in 1998 when I received a rare phone call from Maria. She asked me to come over as soon as I had an opening. Over the weeks, Maria denied continuously that her boyfriend ever hit her children. She was adamant that her children were lying. Since that time, Maria had also enrolled in a back-to-school program. She was studying to become a daycare worker.

That afternoon, at her apartment, in her usual flat tone of voice, Maria told me the following.

'I couldn't sleep you know. It's true what Juan and Gabriella said about Miguel. And I did know. I was just scared. Like I said, my dad hit my brother and sometimes my brother hits his girlfriend. Juan was throwing things so much, and you know it's no good he don't respect no one.

'But I been in school for a few days [she had been in school since the previous October], and I been readin' and thinkin'…and the books say if you hit a child then the child hits back…and I keep rememberin' my dad. You know, I don't know what I'm going to do, 'cause I threw Miguel out, and then he got arrested for drugs, you know. I mean sometimes I smoked the pot with him, you know, but he did more. But my phone might get cut off 'cause, well, I think he was sellin'. Anyway, he had money all the time… and now here I am alone with four children…it's gonna be hard to get respect.

'I asked you to come early before the kids come in, things is changin', kind-of. Everythin' is good, but I am so busy. I have to read all these books and take tests…they is hard. And the kids don't stop fightin' and they don't listen. But something I learned in school…and something from you… I'm beginnin' to listen to the kids. I'm beginnin' to listen to you and to the teacher, you know, kinda of like that guy with the magic cake, what was his

122

name, Anthony? And I think about that other guy, the one who went lookin'
for his wife, sometimes you gotta do things like listen to your kids even if
you don't know what's gonna happen, sometimes it's just better that way.'

Stories and gentler changes

Maria was internalizing the two stories I had told her and using this
internalization to help her come to the truth about her life. The
stories, in combination with her education and the therapy, were all
working within her unconscious to gently melt away the harsh
edges of denial she had lived with for so long. The stories were
providing a safer and kinder way for her to approach the truth.

When she had finished talking, Maria looked up at me, her brown eyes
shining. 'I feel better knowin' all this.'

At that point, all the children came rushing in. They were carrying
empty soda cans, and their excitement shook their small bodies. 'Look how
many, you get five cents for all of them, we found them everywhere...' Juan
couldn't stop talking. I was aware of his ability to lead a group of children in
an enterprise and experience success.

'Where did you find so many soda cans?' I asked, truly impressed.

'Just down there.' Juan pointed in the direction of the street. I surmised
you didn't have to go far, so many of this town's streets were full of litter.

'You know that magic cake? Well, we was looking for magic in the
cans...we was pretendin'...but we really do get money!'

'Well, maybe magic doesn't lie in cakes or cans.'

But the kids were all over me. 'Can we color, can we do stories?'

We sat down in the kitchen, at the little table. Maria joined us.

'Look, you guys. You never listen to me. You know your school
uniforms? You know they is very expensive, and you come home and you
play in your uniforms. All you have to do is change your clothes and hang up
or fold that uniform. I am so sick of tellin' you to do this.'

Gabriella's eyes were shining. 'Okay...now a story, Molly?'

'See what I mean?' Maria looked at me.

'I want to talk with you about *Anthony and the Magic Cake*. How did Anthony listen?'

'I don't know,' Gabriella said.

'He gots a lot of money,' Juan broke in. 'That's what I want…a lot of money.'

'And how did he get a lot of money?'

'The old man.' This from Juan.

'NO! By listening…'

'You mean if you listen you get money? Mom don't have no money. She can't pay me to listen.'

'How valuable is listening, Juan?' I asked.

He shrugged.

'Do you get in trouble when you don't listen? What happens when you do listen?' The children were quiet.

Maria said, 'I listened to you, Juan. I got Miguel to leave.'

'He be bad to me. I'm glad he ain't here.'

'Me too,' said Gabriella.

'Mom is right,' I intervened, 'She did listen to you, Juan. You did a good job of telling.'

'Will you tell another story?' Gabriella asked.

Maria was now standing next to Juan. She had her hand on his head. 'You 's a good kid, Juan. I'm sorry Miguel hit you. I'm sorry I didn' do nothin'.'

'You did, Mom, you made him go to jail.'

Maria sighed. This would be a long story. 'No…he's in jail for drugs. Don't you ever do drugs… But I didn' want him hittin' you no more.'

'Can we have a story?' begged Gabriella, pulling on me.

I remained quiet for just a moment longer. And then I said, 'Today, you all are going to tell me a story.'

They told the following tale, with Maria chipping in here and there. Maria's flat tone actually took on expression as her children participated in the story.

Figure 6. 'The Cat and the Dog with the Magic Hat' by Juan Vera

Figure 7. 'The Cat and the Dog with the Magic Hat' by Gabriella Vera

The Cat and the Dog with the Magic Hat

by Juan, Gabriella, Pedro, Angel, and Maria Vera

In the zoo, a long time ago, the cat and the dog were fighting because they fought all of the time. The cat and dog scratched each other all day long and stole each other's food. When the dog barked the cat got scared. They did this because they were a dog and a cat.

One day, Monsterman came to steal the dog and the cat so he could have a lot of animals, so he could sell them so he could have a lot of money. When Monsterman was sleeping, the lion had a great idea. He would take the dog and cat back because they knew where the magic hat was. They found the magic hat. They made magic with the magic hat and flew back home to the zoo. Now the cat, the lion, and the dog are best friends forever because they don't want to get lost or fight anymore. Monsterman was so mean to them it made them want to stop.

They found the magic hat and wished they could all stop fighting and go home to the zoo. They also wished for the Monsterman never to bother them again. They all ended up at the zoo, and although the cat and dog were more polite to each other, they still argued. However, the lion often came around with the magic hat to help them solve arguments. He asked the magic hat for a bi-lingual teacher. This teacher taught the cat how to bark and the dog how to meow. In this way they learned to get along. This is why it is important to know different languages!

'Does Monsterman remind you of anyone?' I asked everyone in the room.

'YES!' And Juan was jumping up and down in his seat! 'Miguel!'

'And you!' shouted Gabriella to her brother.

'And all of yous guys,' laughed Maria.

'NO!' shouted Juan, 'I wish I had a magic hat!'

'Me too!' said Gabriella.

'Maybe we could talk about magic for a minute.' I interjected.

'Ain't no such thing.' said Maria. 'You have to do everything for yourself; life is just hard hard hard.'

'Mom! I'm gonna listen to you from now on.' This from Gabriella.

'What about that other guy? Did he ever find his girl?' This from Juan.

'What do you think, Juan?'

'Maybe with a lot of hard work, he finally found her,' added Maria.

About stories

Maria Vera's family found hope after hearing the stories I told them. In both stories, the heroes encountered hardship. They both went on long adventures and were led back home in order to discover a truth about themselves. Both Anthony and Tu Thac had to listen to their inner voices.

Tu Thac came back to 'earth' in order to internalize all he had learned from the fairy grotto. Through a good deed, he found love in one aspect of his consciousness. His next task was to unite this other-worldly/spiritual level of consciousness with his earthly self-knowledge. He knew that this type of internal journey was a lifelong process and one well worth engaging in.

In addition, on some deep unconscious level, the children knew a different, more united life existed. Tu Thac's journey confirmed this. Moreover, it was Tu Thac's struggle to find something he had lost, rather than the final result we're never told, that provided the hope. Maria's children knew only too well the suffering of the concrete world. Intrinsically, however, they knew through identification with the heroes in both stories that success was possible, and possible through the very *struggle* itself. They all decided that Tu Thac would find his wife again, because such a struggle would have to have a happy outcome.

Maria understood life on a concrete level, on a level where 'magic' or 'fairy grottos' could never exist. But the very telling of the stories had enabled her to tell her own, and had enabled the children to tell theirs. The process of storytelling unfolded each story and as each story unfolded, more hope was gained. The more hope that was gained, the more hope they could see in each story, and the more hope they would internalize.

Their own tale was an outpouring of this new-found hope. The children knew that all they did was fight with each other. The fighting was becoming a monster that wanted to hurt them. The fighting was also making them feel like caged animals. They were searching for a 'magic' solution to help them stop fighting.

> The very telling of their story indicated to me that they each had the means to gain control of the fighting and become friends. The 'magic' they were looking for to stop the fighting lay right inside their own internal controls. These internal controls were already activated through the hope the stories provided. It was my job to help them manifest the friendship that already existed between them.

'I have an idea,' I said. 'Only, Maria, you need to leave the room!'

'Is it a secret?' asked Gabriella.

'Kind of.'

'Then we can go into my room.'

Juan, Angel, Pedro, Gabriella and I all piled into a bedroom the size of a large closet. Two bunk beds hit each spare wall, and shelves climbed in the spare spaces. Clothing was all over the place, in spite of an attempt to maintain order.

'Listen, you guys, do you want to surprise Mom?'

They all nodded excitedly.

'Well, each day after school until I come again next time, I want you all to sneak into your room, change your clothes, fold or hang your uniforms, and when each of you is all set, hold hands and run into the kitchen to Mom and yell "SURPRISE"! And what will be the surprise?'

'We listened,' said Gabriella. 'We changed our clothes.'

'Right,' I said 'and how will Mom be?'

'Happy.'

'Right. What happens when you listen?'

'Mom don't yell.'

'What happens when you don't listen?'

'Mom yells.'

'Okay, then, pretend you are the cats and dogs who are friends. Remember, you are a team and listening is your magic hat, and not listening is Monsterman! How's about that? And you each have a choice as to which you want to be.'

They all giggled and laughed and ran back into the kitchen to draw pictures to their story.

Everyone was home at the Gonzales house. Ricardo skipped around me as we walked into the living room. I gave them each a copy of the story. Tanya and Ricardo fought to read it out loud.

After they both read it out loud, Ricardo wanted to read it out loud again.

'PLEASE! Moooooolllllleeeeeeeee, can we PLEASE WRITE ANOTHER STORY NOW!!!!'

'Ricardo, why do you behave that way?' Jorge asked, his tone flat and his face blank.

'Ricardo,' Clara had had it. 'You are NEVER polite. Oh, Molly, he does have ADHD, but I never have time to get him the pills at the drugstore, and you know I don't like givin' my kids nothin' like that, and you know he did do his chores this week. It ain't that he don't never listen.'

'I think you should give him that stuff – maybe he's gonna listen better,' Jorge said.

'Why do you think he did his chores?' I asked, surprised.

Clara shrugged and Ricardo didn't know.

I wondered about the process of storytelling. Could these characters, the dragon and the bird, be working in Ricardo to help change his behavior? Could the making of that story with his family have created a deeper connection to himself and to his parents so that he would want to listen?

How could I further help him along? How could I help the family begin to see him more clearly and treat him differently?

ADHD and PTSD

ADHD is difficult to diagnose, especially when there is truama in the family. Post-traumatic stress syndrome (PTSD) can look like ADHD. ADHD is much easier to diagnose in families where there is no history of traumatic abuse. For families like Ricardo's, impoverishment alone is trauma enough, let alone the added stress of being hit with belts, and outbursts of temper.

Recently, I had worked with a nine-year-old child who was now in foster care. When I first met him, he was jumping off the kitchen counters and refrigerator, hitting his siblings and neighbors, running constantly into the street, and riding his bike in dangerous situations. He couldn't have a conversation, and he swore constantly. His home was a shambles, and his mother was actively using drugs and alcohol. With DSS intervention, he was put into foster care.

Two weeks after living in foster care his behavior calmed down and completely changed. Why? He was being fed regularly and at consistent times. It appeared that this boy had not eaten regularly for weeks, and had experienced neglect on many levels. Due to this trauma, he developed behaviors that resembled ADHD. When he was put in a calmer, more nurturing environment all of those symptoms dissipated. He experienced depression and post-traumatic stress, but there was no evidence at all of ADHD.

Ricardo was jumping from the couch and landing just at that table's edge.

'RICARDO!!!'

'WHAT'S ADHD?!' Ricardo was shouting as he kept leaping. Tanya was giggling hard.

'Well, if you sit down a minute, I can tell you,' I attempted. 'Ricardo, remember the dragon in your story?'

'YESSSSSSSSSSSSSSSSSSSSS!' cried Ricardo, taking another flying leap.

'I think we should tell a story,' Tanya giggled.

'Fine,' said Clara, exhausted, 'but you have to take turns.'

'Ricardo,' I said, 'We can't tell a story until you sit down. Here, come sit next to me. Ricardo jumped next to me. 'Ricardo, what do you remember about the dragon in the story?'

'He was sick, just like me! I have somethin' that makes me sick, right?'

Clara's face fell. 'Ricardo, honey, you're not sick...no, you just don't act polite.'

'I think there is somethin' wrong.' Jorge said.

'Ricardo,' I tried again, 'What did the dragon do in your story even though he wasn't feeling well?'

'He yawned and made the bird find the ring! HE KNOCKED THE OLD LADY'S DOOR DOWN!'

'So, even though he wasn't feeling well, he could still do really strong things. You've been doing your chores, you can make everyone laugh when you play with the baby, and you draw beautifully. After you tell another story, I can tell you about ADHD. I want you to be the dragon in the story and think of ways you can help this story along. You tell everyone whose turn it is.'

Ricardo did just that. With some more guidance, he asked the questions I normally ask, and he did a great job. He even insisted that I tell my story response then and there. This is the story the family told, with my response.

Figure 8. 'The Magic Pumpkin' by Ricardo Gonzales

Figure 9. 'The Magic Pumpkin' By Tanya Gonzales

The Magic Pumpkin

by Ricardo, Tanya, Clara, and Jorge Gonzales

Once upon a time in the scary forest, it was midnight on Halloween. The Alien wanted to kill the Ghost, but he couldn't 'cause he'd already died. The Alien also wanted to kill the Werewolf. The Alien wanted to kill the Ghost because the Alien didn't have any candy.

The Ghost and the Werewolf guarded the Magic Pumpkin. The Pumpkin had the power to make people good, and the Alien had the power to make people bad. The Alien wanted to make pumpkin pie out of the Pumpkin and rule the forest. He stole the Pumpkin.

The Werewolf and the Ghost cried because he stole their best friend, the Magic Pumpkin. Everybody was crying because they missed the Pumpkin. Everyone went to the Alien. 'Why did you steal our friend, the Pumpkin?'

'Because I had no candy. Because I am so hungry.'

They gave the Alien ten pieces of candy so he would never take the Pumpkin again. He was so happy with his candy that he gave the Pumpkin back, and everybody was happy again.

Once upon a time, on Halloween, in the forest, a very mean Alien was trying to kill a very wonderful Ghost. The Alien, however, soon needed to give up this attempt because everyone knows you can't kill a ghost — ghosts are already dead. But this did not stop the angry Alien. He decided he would try to kill the Ghost's best friend, the Werewolf, instead.

The Ghost and the Werewolf, you see, were guardians of the Magic Pumpkin. This fabulous Pumpkin had the power to make people good or bad. The Alien wanted the Magic Pumpkin so he could make everybody mean and angry like himself.

'I'd like to make pumpkin pie out of that Pumpkin,' he gloated to himself. 'Yes, and then I could use its power to rule the forest, and everyone will be mean. Ah, what a glorious idea.'

On that fateful night, at midnight on Halloween, the Alien managed to injure the Werewolf. The Ghost was beside himself with grief, and he spent all of his energy trying to heal the Werewolf. It was at this point that the Werewolf was able to steal the Magic Pumpkin.

Everyone in the forest was suddenly very, very sad. The stars stopped shining, and the moon stopped glowing. All of the animals and birds were howling and crying. Finally, the brave and wonderful Ghost, with all of the creatures of the forest following him, approached the Alien.

'Why, oh, why did you steal our wonderful Pumpkin?' The Ghost asked.

'Because I am so hungry, because I want candy so much, and no one will ever give me any.'

The Ghost gave the Werewolf ten pieces of candy so he would never take the Pumpkin again. The Alien was so happy with his candy (this was the first time anyone had ever been kind to him) that he gave the Magic

Pumpkin back. One by one, the stars began to glow again, slowly the moon dried her tears and started to shine, and soon all of the creatures of the forest were happy again.

The Ghost, the Werewolf, and the Alien all guard the Magic Pumpkin, and all over the world, pumpkins welcome these three good and strange folk into their patches to hear the story of the Magic Pumpkin again and again.

After the telling of this story, Ricardo asked, 'Why am I so stupid?'

His mother replied, 'Ricardo, honey, you're not stupid, you're very smart, you just don't listen, and that's what gets you into trouble.'

'Then why does my brain feel mushy when I try to behave right?'

'What do you mean your brain feels mushy?' I asked.

'I don't know, I can't explain it, but when I try to do good I don't.'

'You don't behave poorly on purpose, Ricardo, and you have something called ADHD. You were born with this way of behaving, and the good news is that you have the control to change it. You are already trying. You have that magic pumpkin inside of you, and no alien can hurt it. This is the "magic" inside of you; the "magic" where you can gain control to behave, to listen, to sit still.'

'You think he can?' asked Clara.

'Ricardo, you do good, you know you are a good boy.' Jorge said.

'Ricardo is a wonderful boy.' I said to Jorge. 'You and Clara have done a good job.'

The family system in the story, *The Magic Pumpkin*

In their story, the characters actually *talked* to the alien, and the alien could actually *express* what he needed. The idea of the conversation between the alien and the other characters came from Jorge. The storytelling was teaching Jorge and Ricardo to talk with each other rather than to yell, and as they engaged in this new process of relating to each other, kindness was coming through. They were emulating the friendship between the werewolf and the ghost.

I once again elaborated on this story rather than change the ending. The family was really working through all of the 'alien' parts of their system. In this story they were slowly seeing and befriending those aspects that were negative – all of the meanness, the yelling, the blaming. The ghost and werewolf existed in the system, as well as within each individual. The family was coming together through a new ritual of story making, and in doing so were creating new possibilities for themselves.

CHAPTER NINE

The Blue Moon

Two weeks later, I was at Maria's. A cold March wind was blowing. As usual, the children tumbled all over me as I walked in. I had their story in tow, this time with my ending. They all barked and meowed, and Juan said, 'See, we are trying to get along. We listen to Mom, now!'

'Yeah,' Gabriella said, 'we surprise Mom every day, huh, Mom?'

'Yeah, they bein' good,' Maria said in her flat tone. 'They come home and change and run out of their room and say "surprise."'

'What makes you guys do that?' I asked, as we all sat down at the table. They shrugged their shoulders and immediately delved into drawing as I read their story and my ending. Juan and Gabriella and the other two children began to meow and bark at each other. Maria came into the kitchen to find out what all the noise was about. She managed to help them quiet down, and I watched her in growing amazement.

'Maria, your children are listening better.'

'Yeah, they always good kids, you know. It's just me. I got so many problems. You think you can just come see me? I'm in school and it's a lot of work, and I am workin' at Ame's and my brother don't want to babysit no more.'

The children started barking and meowing again. Juan was laughing hard. 'Look Molly, I'm meowing and Gabriella is barking and before I was barking. I think the magic hat is coloring and stories!'

'Know what I think? I think you're right! And I also think you can be best friends just like the lion and the cat and the dog in your story. I like your story, because the lion, the cat, and the dog do become best friends. I like my story 'cause the bi-lingual teacher helps them understand each other. The big lion that can make this happen is in each of you,' I told them. 'So is

Monsterman and so are the cat and the dog. You just have to choose how you want to behave.'

'Yeah…if you feel mad, just wait until the next day!'

'Wow! Juan, just like Anthony! And then while you are waiting for the next day, find that lion inside you. The lion can be bigger than Monsterman. Therefore, you can get control of your anger.'

'Yeah, Juan!'

'Gabriella, what about you? The lion and Monsterman are in you too, you know.'

'No!'

'Yes!' This from Juan.

Maria asked if she could talk to me alone. We walked back into the living room.

'I'm learnin' lots in school 'bout what you said, 'bout listenin' to the children. I think I understand better how to listen to my kids. But I am tired and mad so much. I remember my father a lot.'

Her voice became quiet. 'I remember walkin' home, and there was like a red house with a garage outback, and my father took me there…and…well, you know…I lost my virginity with him. It happened with other guys after that…I never told no one…and I never knew to talk, no one in my family never did. And Anthony had that old man…and that Chinese guy had his wife, even though he left her…I mean, that's what men do – they hurt you and leave. I don' want that for Juan or none of my sons and I'm learnin' in school that if I listen to them they can do better than that…and…and I want to write my own story and I have a teacher at school who likes my writing.'

I knew that Maria was disclosing sexual abuse for the first time. I knew she was thinking about *Anthony and the Magic Cake* and *The Fairy Grotto*. I also understood that she really didn't want to discuss the sexual abuse then and there. There would be time for that.

'Maria,' I said, 'I am really sorry these things happened to you. Really sorry. I can't believe how hard you struggle. And look how far you've come. You are raising four children by yourself, you kicked out the men who have hurt you, and you are excelling in school. To top all of this, you are also working part-time in a department store as a night manager. Do you have any idea as to what you do and accomplish in a day?'

She beamed. 'Yeah…it been real hard. I have another question?'

'Anything.'

'Will you come to my graduation on Saturday?' (She meant in two weeks.)

'Oh, Maria, I don't think I can,' I answered, preparing to leave. 'I will do my best.'

The boundary problem

I had learned from teachers and supervisors to keep my professional boundaries strict and clear. This job was really challenging all of that. Touched by Maria's invitation to her graduation, I felt that attending would have supported her tremendously. I tried hard to change my obligations for that day, unsuccessfully. Instead, I sent her flowers with a congratulations card. Many a teacher and supervisor would have also disapproved of this gesture. However, I was learning that clear boundaries rise out of the relationship with the client, out of what happens in the moment, rather than academic theories.

At our next meeting, Maria greeted me. She was upset that I hadn't gone to her graduation. 'I really wanted you to come, Molly. I gave a speech and everythin'. And in my speech I thanked everybody, includin' you. I even read my story that I wrote. But thank you for the flowers. When my brother saw them, he said, "What, is she gay or somethin'? Does she like you?"'

Maria's new education had helped her tremendously to understand her children's behavior, and her successes in school certainly gave her the confidence to explore herself. In addition, the stories were working inside of her. She saw how much pleasure her children received from hearing and telling their story and drawing pictures, and when she saw how much joy they received, this in turn helped her feel better about herself as a mother.

'But I knew you wasn't gay…that wasn't it.' Maria continued. 'Sometimes it's too hard to explain, know what I mean?

'And you know what I think, now? I think Tu Thac found his wife. Don't you? But some things, they just don't change and you just can't do nothin' about it.'

I couldn't have agreed more.

'Have a good weekend,' Maria said, as I was leaving. I laughed out loud. It was Tuesday.

That particular afternoon I returned to where I had parked in a small, tight, parking lot across from Maria's home. The exit and entrance were the same, and it was narrow. I pulled out of my space and turned my car in the direction of the exit, when another car pulled into the exit/entrance. I waited patiently for this car to pull back out into the street as he had much more room than I did. In spite of the March wind, my windows were rolled all the way down. As I was waiting, deep in thought as usual, the driver of the car opened his car door and jumped out. He was tall, hefty, his skin the color of raisins. He sauntered toward me, beeper in hand.

'What's up darlin', how come you been waitin' for me?'

'I just need you to back up so I can leave.'

He got closer. 'What did you say?' He pulled out a cell phone.

While he was talking to me, yet another car pulled up behind him. Two more guys got out of the car. 'Trouble, Juan, you got female troubles again?' There was a lot of laughing.

I was enraged and wanted to win this fight. I silently waged a surprisingly heated battle inside my head. I felt my rage take over at the same time the story of *Anthony and the Magic Cake* entered my mind. I remembered especially the line, 'If you are so angry you want to hurt someone, wait until the next day.'

Juan was staring at me. 'What's the matter – you still waitin' on me for what? What would you like, darlin'?'

Something snapped inside of me. I rolled the windows shut and squirmed my way back into the parking space. I waited ten minutes for Juan and his friends to pull into the parking lot so I could finally drive out.

Not exempt from the power of stories

When I was trapped waiting in the parking lot at Maria's, I felt as though my rights had been violated. This was victimization. That young man was saying, 'I am stronger than you: I have a beeper and a cell phone and a bunch of friends much bigger than you, and therefore I have power over you!' He was right. In that moment he did. In the moment when I felt the most angry and victimized, I also remembered a profound message from a story. This message enabled me to do the right thing. At that point, the story became *alive* within me, and I experienced a change of behavior, a change which prevented me from being harmed. These stories were having a similarly powerful effect on Maria's and Clara's families.

I was banging on Clara's door. An unusual amount of garbage bags sat to the right of me. As I stood wondering what they were, Clara opened the door.

The apartment looked half empty, and there were triple the amount of bags inside.

'Hi, Molly, I forgot you were coming. I sent the kids over to my sister. We're movin'. Jorge has another job, and we have to go. Just like that Japanese guy and Anthony. Come on in, I'm sorry about the mess. We just found out two days ago…and I gave my stuff to my sister yesterday. We have to go in a couple of days.'

'How are you doing? I mean, besides being overwhelmed with moving? I am sorry you are leaving… I am glad I caught you so I can say goodbye. Please let the kids know I said goodbye, too.'

'Oh, they are going to miss you. And I still haven't given Ricardo any pills. I just don't want to.'

'Are you moving far?'

'No, just a couple of towns away.'

'You know, I could give you the name of a Chinese herbalist who lives in the next town over. He's discovered a herb which helps with depression and ADHD. It works.'

'My sister told me about natural stuff too. Okay, I will take his name.'

My mouth must have fallen open because Clara asked me what was wrong. I shrugged. 'I'm just surprised that you know about herbs.'

'Oh, it was my grandmother over in Puerto Rico, she was always growin' stuff or buyin' stuff. She always gave me ginger for everything.'

'Well, you will like Dr Woo then. But how is Ricardo doing? And how are Jorge and Ricardo doing?'

'Well, funny enough, Ricardo is doin' better. I asked his teacher for a book about ADHD. I remember you sayin' it was good for kids to know stuff about themselves. He don't think he is sick no more and, boy, is he a good drawer and we still have all the stories we did. I made sure I put them somewhere safe. That was fun, those stories.

'As I said, Molly, life isn't like those stories, but in a funny kind of way, it is. I can't explain it, but I find myself telling Jorge to think before he acts and Jorge tells me to be quiet. But then I see he don't get so mad no more, not like he used too. He kind of leaves the room...and then he tells Ricardo he's been mad and thinkin' and I kind of see Ricardo tryin' to do that now.'

Stories and compassion

Stories break all cultural boundaries. Once heard, they settle so far down into the psyche. The ritual of telling family stories changed the way everyone in the Gonzales family was relating to each other. Neither Clara nor Jorge knew how to express their feelings appropriately, and the community at large was filled with angry victimizers and victims, creating and re-creating a story of great disconnection from human contact. Compassion was lost in this family. The stories brought this back into focus. Would Clara have thought to have asked Ricardo's teacher for a book otherwise?

And hadn't I experienced much compassion in this family already? Jorge had come to every meeting, and participated in both of the stories. There was no question that he did not wish to be an absent father.

With Clara that day I reviewed our work together over the past six months. Her head was down toward the end of the session. She wasn't saying much. We both stood up to say goodbye. She swung her heavy head of hair behind her and looked at me, her brown eyes brimming with tears.

'Thank you, Molly,' she said, taking my hand.

We walked quietly to the door. The lump in my throat was giving way, as Clara waved and shut the door.

PART THREE

The Creation Story

CHAPTER TEN

Fossilized Stars

It was a raw February morning in 1998. I was talking with my colleague, Yvette, a kindergarten teacher in a government-funded program.

'I have a monster girl on my hands,' Yvette said. 'Her name is Ruby. She is a terror, hitting the other children and swearing. Ruby's alcoholic father has been incarcerated often for hitting her mother, and Ruby witnessed this. Recently, the courts awarded him supervised visitations on the weekends.

'Her mom is skinny as a rail – she may be anorexic. She recently had a baby by the same dad, and she hardly ate when she was pregnant. She's suffered extensive abuse, I am sure. I only know half of it, but I'm calling 'cause you gotta get over there and help poor Ruby, what a terror.'

I was already half an hour late for Anna Costava's appointment. I had been circling her neighborhood for that long looking for her apartment. Many of the apartment buildings were boarded up, and some looked charred as though fires had hit them. The streets were littered and crowded, and I wondered where all of these people lived. They were probably living illegally in these condemned homes, rent free. Very few of the buildings had numbers on them. I finally drove away from the area searching for a pay phone.

I stopped at several phones before I could find one in working order. It took Anna forever to answer the phone. 'Should we reschedule?' I asked, hearing a baby screaming.

'What? I can't hear you. Are you coming?'

'Yes.' I realized that Anna probably had no idea I was so late. 'But I can't find your home. Can you give me better directions?'

'It's the green-brown door between the two black ones, right on Lawrence Street.'

There were no street signs. I asked for landmarks, which took Anna a while to describe to me.

'My buzzer don't work. How long before you come?'

'Twenty minutes.'

'Okay, Ruby will wait for you.'

I finally found the apartment. The entire building looked shut down. It was solid stone and a few of the windows were boarded up. The green-brown door was a huge metal hunk, menacing and heavy. I rang the buzzer and knocked, hoping somebody inside would hear.

A little peanut of a girl lugged open the huge door. She was probably no more than three feet tall and must have weighed 30 pounds. She had short brown hair, sharp sparkling brown eyes, and she was wearing an umpire blue dress with great flare.

'Hi,' I said, bending down to shake her little hand. 'I'm Molly.'

'Well, I'm Ruby, and you can only come in if I say so.'

'Oh, well, I think your mother knows…'

'RUBY! What are you doin'? Show the lady how to come up!'

'Well,' said Ruby, 'you *may* come up now. What do you have in your hands? What's in that box? You have to show me now. You have to.'

'I will as soon as we get inside, okay?'

We walked right into the kitchen of the small two-bedroom apartment. It was a little round room with a huge pot of beans and pork bubbling on the stove. Spilled sauce, bones, pieces of discarded onion and meat were scattered across the surface of the stove and floor. The sink was piled high with cooking spoons, plates, and cups.

Baby clothing and bottles, both clean and dirty, were scattered in the corners of the room, and a broken doll lay at the entrance between the kitchen and living area. The overall smell was of dirty diapers, onion, and soured milk.

Anna was sitting at the table, her long skinny arms holding her infant. Her face was pale, and her dyed blonde hair was pulled back into a ponytail. When she greeted me, her voice was flat, and her eyes looked drawn and pulled into their sockets, as though the very life had been dried out of her.

'Have a seat. Ruby's teacher told me she was gonna call DSS. I just got rid of them, you know, and she was gonna call them if I didn' agree to have you come over. It's all because of her,' she nodded in the direction of Ruby. 'I keep tellin' her "don' hit nobody" and she still does.'

I was feeling uncomfortable talking about Ruby in front of her.

'How's about Ruby and I meet together alone right now, and maybe you and I could meet alone when Ruby isn't home?'

'Sure, go right ahead. Ruby, go on now, show Molly to your room. That ways you can have some privacy.'

When we were in Ruby's room, she shut the door and told me I couldn't leave until she told me to. It was surprisingly tidy. Cardboard boxes, lined up against one wall, were filled with dolls, doll clothing, old games, pieces of paper, broken crayons, dried markers, books, outgrown clothing, and dirty laundry. Her dresser was old but clean, and shirts and pants hung over the edges, as the drawers couldn't close properly. The pink bedspread was faded and worn thin. It bore the Barbie logo. We sat on her floor. She opened the box of crayons, but didn't touch any of them.

'Do you know why I'm here?' I asked.

Ruby nodded. 'I know I am bad at school.'

'What do you mean, "bad"?'

She wouldn't answer the question. Instead, she gave me more directions. 'You have to draw now, you have to.'

Understanding the effects of domestic violence

Ruby was demanding. She also frightened her peers, whom she could easily manipulate and control.

Why did she need so much control? Perhaps much of her short-lived experiences included watching her father reel out of control, hitting and yelling. Was she therefore doing everything in her power to control her own environment? If she were a witness, and maybe a victim of domestic violence, she could be unconsciously imitating the victimizer when she couldn't get her own way. She could be potentially hitting others when she felt out of control. The birth of the new baby might have had an influence on her too, as well as her mother's unconscious demands and expectations of her.

'Ruby, how would you like to hear a story?'

'What kind of story? A true story?'

'I'll tell you what – you tell me if you think it's true after I tell it.'

'Okay. After you tell the story, you have to draw. You have to.'

I told her *The Creation Story.*

The Creation Story[1]

from the Midrash

A long time ago, Adam and Eve were in their garden. The days were warm, the sky blue, and the trees always ripe with delicious fruits. The aromas of flowers mixed with the juicy smells of dripping peaches, oranges, and plums scented the air. The magenta, purple, orange, yellow, and white flowers mingled with the colors of the river. Everything was completely gorgeous. That is, until the snake (who, by the way, walked on two legs at the time) told Eve to eat a pomegranate, the very fruit God told them *not* to eat.

'Come on, Eve, God won't know,' urged the snake. And when the snake broke open the pomegranate, Eve was thrilled. The skin inside the hard, red rind was pure white, and bright red seeds were tucked between. 'See,' said the snake, 'you simply eat it like this.' And the snake showed Eve what to do. Eve saw that nothing happened to him. So she decided to have some too. What a taste! Holding onto the pomegranate Eve ran to Adam.

'Look at this!'

'Eve! That's the pomegranate, the fruit that God told us not to…'

'Yes, but it's delicious, and nothing has happened to me. Go on, Adam, have some.' And he did, and he too found the food wonderful.

But all of a sudden, Adam and Eve were looking at each other funny. They blushed and they ran and put fig leaves around themselves. However, at this time, they heard God, and He was angry.

'Adam, Eve, Snake, what have you done? You have broken a rule and you are all responsible. For this, Snake you shall lose your legs and the mud will be your bed. As for you, Adam and Eve, the two of you must leave this garden forever. Tomorrow at this time you must leave. But just as you lock the gates forever, I will give you a gift. This gift will make you feel much better.' Throughout the day and night Eve and Adam said goodbye to all of the animals and plants that they had come to love so dearly. The next morning, the pair walked out of the garden. They locked the gate together. Adam and Eve looked at one another. Eve put her hand gently on Adam's cheeks. They were soaking wet, although there was no rain. Clear, funny-shaped water was dripping from his eyes and falling down his cheeks. Softly, Eve wiped the water from his face. Adam saw the same funny-shaped water falling from Eve's eyes. He, too, gently put his hand on her cheeks, wiping the water away. All of a sudden, Adam hugged Eve, and they sobbed in each other's arms. They were sorry they had disobeyed God, and they were sorry they had to leave this beautiful place. They were grateful they had each other, and frightened and excited about their future. They cried in each other's arms for a long time. When the tears stopped, they felt much better. Holding hands, they turned and looked to the horizon. The sun was high in the blue air. The desert was all around them. They heard God. 'Yes, Adam, yes, Eve; you see, I have given you the gift of tears. Whenever you feel sorry, excited, or grateful for something, or whenever your chest feels tight, use this gift of crying. It will make you feel so much better. Go now, be on your way, I will always be with you.'

'What did you think of that story?'

'Good. Look, I have a doll. You want to see her?'

Ruby stood on her tiptoes and pulled down a doll in a plastic box. She was porcelain, with brown eyes and black lashes. Her hair was brown, and bangs fell across her forehead. She was wearing a white pinafore over a green gingham checked dress, with brown shoes.

'Oh!' I said, 'She is beautiful! Who gave that to you?'

'My Nana. But Mom got mad.'

'Why?'

'She told my Nana that it was too much money, that she could use the money for the baby and that I would break it anyway. And Mom told me I could never take her out of the box, so you can't. You can only look at her, see?'

'Ruby,' I said, 'you know it is almost time for me to go. Thank you so much for showing me your special doll. She really is beautiful, and I am glad you are taking such good care of her. I would like to come back and see you.'

'You can only come over if I tell you. And you can't leave yet. I said you *can't*.' Ruby followed me out of the bedroom and into the kitchen continuing to give me orders. She made a beeline for the baby lying in his sleeper and immediately began to rock it, a little bit too hard.

'Ruby, you leave that baby alone. You're going to make him cry; now leave him alone.' Anna's tone was flat, passive, and completely ineffective. Ruby paid no attention. The baby woke up and cried.

Anna picked up her son. She made a gesture to hit Ruby and sat down with the infant without saying a word to her daughter. Ruby picked up a stool and set it by the sink. She climbed on top of it and soon the sink water was running and soap bubbles were forming. Anna continued to ignore her, and quickly the soap bubbles were reaching the edge of the sink. I walked over and turned off the water.

'Maybe you can...'

'YOU CAN'T TELL ME WHAT TO DO!' screamed Ruby at the top of her lungs, and she stood on the stool. Her little fist, which was holding the kitchen faucet, dug into mine. Anna turned around to look at Ruby and me. She shrugged and turned away.

'Ruby, get down off that stool. Leave Molly alone.'

I walked over to Anna and told her I would call her. She looked way too tired to schedule another appointment.

I looked at Ruby. 'It was nice meeting you,' I said. 'Thanks again for showing me your doll.'

No one said a word as I walked out the kitchen door.

On induction

When Ruby began to overflow the sink with water, I attempted to discipline Ruby because Anna did not. Anna's passive defense was manifesting as neglect, and this neglect made Ruby scream for attention in any way she could. The more Ruby screamed for attention, the more passive and neglectful Anna became. I jumped in to prevent a disaster, but what I was really doing was taking over the parenting role. Anna would perceive me either as an adult in charge, and therefore someone not to be trusted, or she would perceive me to be on Ruby's 'side.' Either way, her passiveness toward me could only increase.

What would have happened if I had not interfered? What would have happened if I had allowed things to take their course, which they do when I am not around? It would have been better, perhaps, to allow Anna and Ruby to work this issue through – to allow them to have their own experiences. After all, isn't that what the creation story is all about?

Two weeks later I met Nancy. Nancy, like Ruby, had a father who was actively abusing substances. When I first met her, she was living with her grandparents, who were also her foster parents. She was living with them until her mother, Lynn, could meet all of DSS demands. These included the following: leave her husband, attend AA meetings and parenting education classes, and engage in both individual and family therapy. In addition, I was asked to give eight-year-old Nancy Rizzo individual therapy, especially since reunification was pending and almost certain.

According to the DSS worker, Lynn Rizzo was working hard to accomplish the above-mentioned goals. DSS thought that the father was still in the picture, but they knew he was no longer living with her.

Both Nancy and her younger sister, Linda, greeted me at the door of their grandmother's apartment and led me into the living room. Toys covered the plush brown rug. The grandmother was in the kitchen. She yelled to me to 'make yourself at home, and talk with the girls.' The smell of garlic and onion seeped into the room as we sat on the comfortable, deep blue couch.

I couldn't have met two more different looking sisters. Linda was small in stature, had pale skin, pale blue eyes, and almost white-blonde hair, which was straight and long. She wore a bright blue headband, which matched the color of her tee shirt. Her jeans were neat and clean, as was her entire appearance.

Nancy looked as though she were ten or eleven years old. She was stocky, tall, and darker skinned. Her hair was brown-black, short, and wavy. She wore a red and green striped shirt with purple and pink checked pants; they were filthy at the knees, as though she had been kneeling in the dirt looking for bugs and other treasures.

Nancy was aggressive and verbal, and Linda was quiet, though probably suffering as well, perhaps in a passive-aggressive manner.

From dysfunctional to functional

In a dysfunctional family, the quiet child usually suffers as much as the aggressive child. Unconsciously, children take on different roles in the family as a means of acting out the dysfunction, and as a means of self-preservation. The child who placates or remains quiet so as to be 'invisible,' does so in order to keep the one she is placating from becoming angry with her.

The Rizzos were deeply stuck in their dysfunctional roles: Nancy as the lonely, aggressive child, and Linda as the quiet one. Paradoxically – as is true in all families – there is just as much possibility for becoming functional as there is for being dysfunctional. The necessary opposites always exist together, even though we cannot always see this. For example, the moon and the sun shine at the same time even though we cannot actually see this. Our bodies are filled with positive and negative electrons. These opposing forces make it possible for our physical bodies to function properly. So it is with our feelings and our beliefs. We can feel despair in one moment, and hope in another. Objectively, however, these two feelings exist at the same time. If you are feeling despair, you can ask yourself, where is my hope? And eventually you will be able to feel hope. At the moment you are feeling hope, you can ask yourself, where is my despair? And you will be able to feel it. If you ask yourself to feel both at the same time, you will be able to see that this is possible.

So if the functionality and the health in the Rizzo family was there along with the dysfunction, how could I help them realize this potential?

'Nice to meet you, Molly.' Mrs Constantine emerged from the kitchen. Whiffs of basil, garlic, and tomato steamed from her body. She was a short, stocky woman with grey cropped hair. 'Go right ahead, make yourself comfortable. You can work with Nancy. I'll take Linda into the kitchen with me. Come on darlin', you can help me bake cookies in just a few...'

As Mrs Constantine took Linda by the hand, Linda turned around, stared at Nancy and made the ugliest face I have ever seen.

'STOP IT, YOU STUPID IDIOT!' screeched Nancy, at the top of her lungs. She used a high-pitched tone that could have shattered glass.

'Nancy!' reprimanded Mrs Constantine. 'I'm sorry, Molly, but now you see how things are.' Linda skipped into the kitchen with her grandmother.

Nancy led me into her bedroom. There were two beds with the same pink bedspreads and white lace pillow cases. Linda's side of the room was 100 per cent neater than Nancy's. Nancy was pushing school papers, pens, broken pencils, and pencil shavings off her bed, and onto the floor. When I indicated there would be more room on the floor to sit than on her bed, she simply pushed the pile of junk under the bed to make room.

We sat down on the floor and she began to immerse herself in drawing and decorating immediately. 'Nancy, do you know why I'm here?'

'Because Mom says I argue all of the time.'

'Well, do you?'

'No! Everyone always argues with me. No one ever listens to me.'

'No one listens to you?'

'No. I told that social person...'

'Your DSS worker?'

'Yeah…her…that she wasn't the boss of me or my mom, and that Linda and I had a right to live with Mom, and Mom with us.'

'So you want to live with Mom again?'

'Of course! Wouldn't you if you were taken away?'

'This is hard. Do you know why you're not living with Mom?'

'Yes, because I don't listen.'

'Do you think it's because you don't listen?'

'Not exactly. It's because no one listens to me. One time when Dad was living with us there was a whole bunch of people over, and they were all in the bathroom with Dad. And I had to go really badly and I kept banging on the door, and Mom kept hollerin' at me to wait, and I kept screamin' to please listen to me that I really had to go, and then Linda started to cry 'cause she had to go really bad too…and then Mom was hollerin' at me 'cause I made Linda cry. And then both of us peed on the floor and Mom was really hollerin' then callin' me a stinkin' pig but she didn't listen.'

Why abused children want to go back home

Children love their parents unconditionally. When they are removed from their parents' home, no matter how horrendous the conditions, they feel displaced, unloved, and lost. The new environment, even if it is familiar (such as a relative's house), becomes unfamiliar because living there is different from visiting. The rules, the relationships, and sometimes the schools change, and often these changes are sudden. While the new environment is, in fact, safer for the child, the child can begin to feel more unsafe, because the rules and routine have changed so drastically. This change, in combination with how much the child loves the parents, makes the child long for the parent. Often the child will then create fantasies around how much better the parent is than the relative taking care of them, which creates more emotional pain within the child by separating him from his realities. The relative may then feel resentment toward the child, who appears to be 'ungrateful.' Thus, an unending cycle begins: the more resentful the relative, the more angry and hurt the child becomes. This familiar cycle, of course, continues to send the child into the fantasy that her 'real' mom or dad is far better than this person could ever be.

Paradoxically, if the relative sees these fantasies as the child's very struggle to understand his circumstances (and also perceives the resulting dynamic between child and relative), the relative can then create a safe atmosphere for the child to express his feelings, no matter how rude or angry they may be. In this safer place, the child is able to vent the anger he has toward his parents onto the relative, and can eventually connect more deeply to the relative by moving away from fantasies about his parents.

'Nancy, I'm so sorry you went through that. I wonder what that was like for you.'

'Bad. But Mom said sorry the next day, and I did too and it's not so bad.'

'I'm sorry no one listens to you. You know, that reminds me of a story. Would you like to hear it?'

'What kind of a story?'

'Can I surprise you? You can tell me what you think about it in the end.'

I told her *The Creation Story.*

'That was okay. I think God should have given Adam and Eve some food to take with them, not tears. That's weird. He should have given them food, so they wouldn't starve.'

The story had already reached her innate sense of empathy and kindness. Her insights taught me how much she wanted to be seen for her intelligence and generosity.

I told her our time was up, and she protested. She continued to color, begging for more time. I felt irritated, and I understood why her elders grew impatient. Then I realized that I had not given her enough warning about stopping. I gave her another ten minutes to finish up, letting her know at the five-minute mark my expectations. She finished up on time, showing me that she had the capacity to listen, once given some respect herself.

Nancy led me into the kitchen, and I asked to speak with Mrs Constantine in private. I talked with her about my impressions of Nancy, and asked her if she knew about Linda's tactics.

'Oh, I didn't realize she had done that. But...' she gave a long, deep sigh. 'It really doesn't matter. Nancy doesn't listen to anyone and that screechy yell she gives is blood-curdling. And, you know, it really isn't her fault. She is so much like her mother, even looks like her when her mother was that age. Her mother never listened to me. She was into drugs at 13, and sleeping around by 14, and meeting that no-good man of hers who got her into more drugs, and then the pregnancies. And do you think her mother listens now? Always mad, always asking her dad and me for money. She's never been able to keep a job or a home. She's always being evicted, the phone is always shut down, and now her kids are my responsibility. Ach. I am tired. I just wanted to be a grandma not a mother again. I've done that.'

Grandparents as foster parents

Mrs Constantine's position as a foster parent was common in this town. Many grandmothers felt blessed to have a second chance at parenting. They felt that their grandchildren 'redeemed' them from all of their parenting mistakes. The court had many cases pending where parents were refusing to allow grandparents to see their children, and grandparents had declared 'grandparent rights.'

Mrs Constantine explained that her grandparent rights were being exploited in the other direction. 'I feel robbed of being a grandmother. What happened to old-fashioned grandmother-hood? You know, where I can take the grandchildren for an afternoon, give them ice cream and send them home? Now *that's* grandparent's rights

---

Later that afternoon, I was sinking into the black couch in Mrs Cruz's home. Mrs Cruz was sinking into the matching love seat across from me. She, like Mrs Constantine, was a stout, short woman, with white-streaked black hair that was oiled and slicked back tightly, into a long stiff ponytail down her back. Her jet-black eyes were round as moons, and several dimples unfolded around her mouth each time she smiled.

We both sank so deep into the furniture that our feet dangled, unable to reach the floor. I compensated by tucking my feet underneath me, asking first permission to take off my shoes!

Mrs Cruz lived in the Dominican Republic and had come to this town in order to complete the adoption papers for her two grandchildren, Maria and Roberto. Unlike Mrs Constantine, she was elated. She was viewing this adoption as a redemption, as a way to make up for her parenting mistakes. While she didn't say this, she did remark that 'God is good – He is giving me my grandchildren to take care of. Ay Dios, pobrecitos.' (Oh God, poor babies.) She often mixed Spanish with her English, and sometimes her accent was so thick it was difficult to understand her.

'Ay, pobrecitos. Their parents, I don't know what happened. You see, my son he has many problems, drugs, alcohol, and too many women. And the DSS, he looked for the mother, but couldn't find her. And my son is gone too much from the house and the children are too much alone. And so DSS called me in Dominican and told me to come. So of course, I come here. But it is Roberto. He doesn't listen to no one, ever. He doesn't listen to his teachers either. Look, they are coming!'

Two of the most beautiful children I have ever seen burst into the room. Maria, aged six, was the spitting image of her grandmother. She had the same moon-shaped, deep black eyes with matching eyelashes longer than her little finger. Her hair, also slicked back and oiled, was the color of her eyes, and so thick and long that it fell in bunches down to her waist. Wisps of hair also escaped from its hold, and fell in front of her shoulders and over her forehead. Roberto, aged seven, was of stocky build, with coffee-brown eyes shaped like almonds, and thick tufts of curls that spilled around his head. Both children were graced with dimples deepening into the corners of their mouths as they laughed. Their eyes sparkled, making their joy contagious and their presence endearing. Mrs Cruz hugged them both warmly, and sent them into the kitchen for a snack.

When they were done munching, she marched them back into the living room, and quietly withdrew. We settled comfortably on the floor, and when I asked them why they thought I was there, Roberto said, 'So we could color!' and Maria said, 'Because you wanted to meet us.'

I agreed to both answers and asked if they could think about another reason.

Maria raised her hand with gusto. 'Because Roberto doesn't listen!'

'Do so.'

'Don't.'

'Do so, 'cause you're not listenin' now...'

'Like you're not...like this...'and Roberto shoved Maria ever so gently.

'No, like this ...' and Maria shoved Roberto back just a little harder.

I could see this playful interaction escalating very quickly into a full-fledged fight.

'Hey...do you guys want to hear a story?' I took advantage of the sudden pause.

'Here's the rule. You guys can color, but I need you to listen, 'cause I don't want you to miss a single part of the story.'

I launched into *The Creation Story* before they could protest.

'I like God.' Roberto said.

'Me too.' said Maria. 'He's nice.'

'Why is cryin' a present?' Roberto asked after a time.

'Yeah!' agreed Maria. 'You always got beat if you cried.'

'Beat? Maria?'

'Yeah. Dad was always comin' home late wakin' Roberto up makin' him fix him somethin' to eat. And sometimes Dad beat Roberto if he didn' wake up and then he whipped him more for bein' a girl...'

'Being a girl?'

'Yeah. Only girls cry.'

Roberto was not participating in this conversation. His head was down and he had stopped drawing.

'Roberto.' I said softly, 'I want you to know something. I have only just met you, and I know that you have not done anything so wrong that you deserved to be hit. I am so sorry such a terrible thing happened to you, and I will do all I can to help you feel better.'

Roberto smiled. 'Can we talk about somethin' else?'

Guiding children to talk about trauma

Children want to feel happy all of the time. Their natural developmental process calls for play, not for discussing feelings. When I brought up Roberto's abuse, I knew that he was uncomfortable with the subject matter, that the feelings of shame he was experiencing were too big for him to handle. I realized that he was trying to set a boundary around these uncontrollable, sad feelings, which were innately contradictory to his developmental process. Paradoxically, I also knew that by naming and talking about them, he'd begin to feel truer joy. So, what was appropriate right then?

I once had a supervisor who asked me, 'Can you hold for the client what you know about him, and gently guide him toward that knowing within himself? Can you know about his innate goodness without naming it for him, allowing him to have his own experiences, and through his own mistakes, arrive at this same knowing, even if it takes him a lifetime, and even if you are not there as his guide in the end?'

What would be best for Roberto was not forcing the situation; this would not help him. When he asked to change the subject he was saying that he'd had enough, and that I needed to know his limitations as well as his limitless abilities.

'What would you like to talk about, Roberto?'

'I don't know.'

Maria looked at me. 'We're goin' with Grandma, and we're goin' to a beautiful garden. That's what she has at her house.'

'Yeah...' Roberto beamed again. 'Like Adam and Eve, only I hope Grandma won't tell us to leave.'

'Let's call her in.'

When Mrs Cruz appeared, I said to her, 'Show me with your hands how much you love Roberto and Maria.'

Mrs Cruz spread her arms wide. 'More than the moon,' she said.

'Roberto, Maria, show me with your arms how much you love Grandma.'

They spread their arms out wider than wide and Mrs Cruz embraced them with hugs and kisses.

I made another appointment to see them, and left.

Note

1 *A Most Precious Gift* from *Sidrah Stories: A Torah Companion,* by Steven M. Rosman (1989). Retold here by Moly Salans as *The Creation Story.*

CHAPTER ELEVEN

Mars

In the two weeks that followed, I received phone calls both from DSS and Lynn Rizzo. Reunification was in full swing, and a family meeting was arranged at the YMCA where the girls were attending after-school care. I walked into the old YMCA building and followed the hand-printed signs in blue marker to the day care. The large gym was packed with tables and children, and their voices ricocheted against the walls and the cathedral-high ceilings. One of the day care providers pried both Linda and Nancy from their tables and brought them over to me. She led us into the kitchen, saying this was the only space available and was no longer in use. Lynn Rizzo was on time, and the four of us sat waiting for Kevin.

'He's fuckin' late again.' Lynn said angrily.

I opened my mouth to say something, but Nancy beat me to it.

'Mom, you shouldn't swear.'

'Don't talk back to me, young lady. I'm too tired for this. He's always fuckin' late and he's fuckin' late with his paycheck too. That's why he's not comin'. I'm gonna lose the apartment because of him.'

Linda was quiet. She was leaning back in her chair silently.

'Mom, you're swearing again, and I hate that and...'

'Nancy, shut the fuck up.'

'Nancy, Lynn. You guys, this isn't productive.'

'And you can talk to me when you've done cleanin' your room, and helpin' me out with the fuckin' mess in the kitchen.' I sat back and watched helplessly.

Parentified children

Nancy had taken on her mother's job because she had spent so many years taking care of her mother. Her argumentive stance was a defense that covered her own guilt around not being able to make her mother happy.

Lynn, of course, was acting out of her own guilt and shame and not facing herself or the consequences of her choices. By refusing to face these consequences, she was also relinquishing her job as parent, and since someone needed to take on that family role, Nancy unconsciously decided to do so. Unfortunately, the more she did this, the more her anger intensified – and the more her anger intensified, the more she parented. This was the way she learned to communicate with her parents, and by remaining in this role, she received much attention, albeit negative.

Kevin and Lynn, on the other hand, were refusing to acknowledge their own behavior and continued to punish Nancy for hers. If they could face their shame and guilt instead, they would feel stronger. But by allowing Nancy to take it on, their guilt was increased. As the family habitually engaged in their inappropriate roles, Nancy was also internalizing her parents' behavior and acknowledging it as normal on an unconscious level. This internalizing, along with the role she was taking on, would most likely lead her to behave the same way as an adult as her mother was behaving now.

Kevin walked in. His presence was magnetic: a tall, stocky man with jet-black hair which cascaded down his face and chin and was also pulled back into a ponytail. His blue workshirt and worn jeans were stained with tar and dirt, and his large, calloused hands were no less stained. He sauntered toward us, and tousled both Linda and Nancy's hair, their cheeks blushing with pleasure.

Before Lynn could open her mouth, he tossed a check in front of her, folded into a tiny square.

He sat down and said, 'Hey, sorry I'm late, the work you know. So many hassles. Hey, kids how are you guys?'

'What happened to last week's check?' Lynn interrupted, 'This isn't fuckin' enough and you want to come home with *this*?' Her voice was entering a screech much like Nancy's.

'Mom, stop your fuckin' swearin' ...'

'NANCY, THIS IS NONE OF YOUR FUCKIN' BUSINESS, SHUT THE FUCK UP FOR THE LAST FUCKIN' TIME!'

'Hey, Lynn, cool it, babe. Jeeze, I've been workin' so much.'

'Yeah, the fuck you have. How much did you spend on your drugs, huh? Or was it that fuckin' whore you used to hang out with?'

'Dad, what's a whore? And are you going to make us leave the apartment?'

Nancy jumped in. 'Mom just got it, and it ain't right if we have to go again, and Mom is workin' and goin' to school and you have to help too.'

I finally intervened and I told them the following Native American story.

How the Bat Came to Be[1]

A Native American Tale

Many years ago, in the northeastern woodlands, on this particular spring morning, Bear woke up, and boy, was he hungry. His stomach was rumbling, and he couldn't wait to find breakfast. But when he stepped out of his cave, he stood still in shock, for it was pitch black. He was scratching his head, when he heard Eagle flying above him.

'Hey, Eagle,' Bear whispered.

'What is it, Bear?' Eagle asked, flying around him.

'Are you as hungry as I am?'

'I sure am.'

'What do you suppose has happened to Sun? Why hasn't he risen?'

'Maybe he's lost!' replied Eagle. 'Let's call a meeting.'

So Bear and Eagle gathered all of the animals together in order to figure out what to do about missing Sun. When all of the animals were gathered, Bear said, 'Since I am the largest animal in the forest, I am going to look for Sun. And when I find him, I will stand to my highest height, and place Sun right back where he belongs.'

But Eagle objected. 'Excuse me, Bear,' Eagle said, 'but I can fly the highest, I have the sharpest vision, and Sun and I share the same home. I think I had better find Sun.'

At that moment, Bear felt something tickling his toes. He looked down and there was Squirrel. 'Excuse me, Bear, excuse me, Eagle,' said Squirrel, 'but I think I had better look for Sun. I can run the fastest and I can climb very high, and I think I am the best equipped.' All of the animals clapped and cheered and so Squirrel was chosen to find Sun.

'Okay,' said Bear, 'but remember, little brother, it is dark, and if you get scared, or too hungry you come right on back.'

Squirrel had already taken off. He ran to the very edge of the forest to climb the tallest tree. From there he would scout from the tip of the tallest branch, and find Sun. However, when Squirrel reached the top of that tree, there was Sun, stuck between its branches. When Sun had tried to rise that morning, he had miscalculated the distance, and become caught between the tree branches.

'OOOOOOOOOHHH, my rays,' moaned Sun, 'my rays, how they ache. Who goes there? Is that you, little Squirrel? Don't come too close, I could burn you. Go get Eagle or Bear.'

'Oh no,' said Squirrel, 'I have come to help you, Sun. With my great teeth, I can chop these branches right down.' Squirrel set to work immediately. Branch after branch fell off, and some of Sun's rays were freed.

'Oh Squirrel,' moaned Sun, 'that feels so good, quick quick, to the left, over here, over here…'

Just in that moment, Squirrel felt a terrible pain down his back. He turned to look, and he saw that all of his beautiful brown fur had been burnt off. 'Oh, big Sun, I am coming to chop off more branches, even though my fur is all gone.' And Squirrel set to work once more. Many more branches fell away, and Sun was becoming impatient. 'Oh, Squirrel, quickly over here, over here…' Squirrel felt another horrible pain right at his tail, and when he looked around he saw that his tail had been completely burnt off. 'I am coming, Big Sun, don't you worry…only my tail has been burnt away.' But Sun was excited, he was almost free! 'Up here, dear Squirrel, just a few more branches. Quickly, quickly!'

However, Squirrel looking upward toward Sun's voice, realized he could not see the rays, or the branches. He had lost his vision. 'Don't you worry, Big Sun, you'll be free in no time, even though I can no longer see.' And, true to his word, Squirrel chopped down the last branches, and Sun was free. He bounced up into the sky, and was so excited he did an elated Sun dance. 'Oh, thank you,' he sang joyously, 'Oh, thank you, little brother, for saving me, the Earth, and all of the animals and plants. Oh thank you!' And Squirrel could have sworn he heard Bear and Eagle clapping.

'Excuse me, Big Sun,' Squirrel finally interrupted. 'I mean, what about me? That is, I really wanted to save you, and I'm really happy I did, but... you know, my beautiful brown fur is gone, my tail has been burnt off, and I can't see.'

'You are so right, little brother,' replied Sun. 'Of course, you have done a grand deed today, and for that I will reward you. Tell me Squirrel, what is it that you have always wanted? I will grant you one wish.'

Squirrel thought for a long time, and then he said, 'I have always wanted to fly.' No sooner said, than Squirrel felt his little body shrink, and his front paws turn into soft leathery black wings. Squirrel practiced flying, but he kept bumping into things, because he couldn't see. 'Excuse me, Big Sun,' Squirrel said. 'I love my wings and everything, but I can't see, and what if I fly right into Bear's belly or land in Eagle's nest and she thinks I'm lunch?'

'Oh,' laughed Sun, 'I'm sorry, little Squirrel. I am going to give you another gift. I am going to give you a new name. From now on, you will be called Bat. It will always hurt you to look at me during the day, and so you will have the pleasure of flying under the moon and around the stars. From now on, you will fly through the dark and sleep during the day. But always remember this, little Bat, as you fly through the darkness, you will always carry my light inside of you.'

Everyone was silent. I wondered when the last time such silence filled the spaces between them.

'All I know,' Lynn said, 'is that I would not sacrifice my life for you, and that was a pretty stupid story, Molly – no one does that, you know, go blind to save someone.'

'If you were so sick, Mom, and needed me to do somethin' like that, I would.'

'Oh, I don't think so. No one would do that.'

'If you lost your kids, Lynn, wouldn't you do anything to find them, to help them?'

'Why do you think I've been workin' so fuckin' hard? They should have never been taken from me in the first place and if this bozo over here would do his part…'

'Lynn, do you believe that everyone has to do their part?'

'I am doin' my part, it's just fuckin' hard when he doesn't do his. I can't do everything.'

'Lynn, if it means doing everything, you will. Look, you can spend the rest of your life blaming and not facing up to your responsibilities, or you can spend the rest of your life looking for a way to take full responsibility, even if it means doing everything. In that way, you set an example for your children, and because you love them you will do whatever you need to do in order to show them that. Blaming is not the way to responsibility.'

Time was up. Everyone was quiet. I made another appointment and said my goodbyes.

It would be two months before I saw the Rizzos again. Lynn was abusing alcohol and the children were back with their grandmother. Mrs Constantine was not returning my calls, and Lynn's phone had been disconnected. I was in touch with DSS, who gave me frequent updates.

Getting drawn into the family dynamics

My direct way of speaking about responsibilities may have been way too much for Lynn. Was she ready to hear all of that? What had happened to that 'holding position' I was able to have and implement with Roberto? What was it about the Rizzo family that caused me to forget myself in that way?

What role had I unwittingly assumed? And how had I been dragged in so quickly into the family dynamics? I jumped in to rescue Nancy. I became impatient with Lynn and Kevin and the way they were speaking, and I was feeling inadequate and unheard because no one was taking my direction. Instead of seeing how inadequate and out of control I was feeling, and facing those feelings, the way I asked Lynn to face hers, I unintentionally acted from these feelings. In so doing, the intervention I used was the exact role Nancy used, and I inappropriately became the authority figure. I took on Nancy's role to rescue her, which would only make her want to rescue her mother from me and I would then become the target of blame. And it was probably for this reason I ended the session so promptly. I had taken on Nancy's role, and by doing this, I understood more clearly the difficulty of her position. Paradoxically, I also understood more clearly the difficulty of Lynn's position. Anyone taking on any kind of authoritative position in this family was never heard.

It was a month later, a gorgeous April afternoon. This was my sixth time at Ruby's. She had heard several stories by now, including *Lady Ragnell, The Fairy Grotto, Anthony and the Magic Cake* and *How the Bat Came to Be*. Her behavior at school was calming down, although Anna reported she was still defiant and hitting the baby.

'Molly, what are you doing with Ruby?' My colleague called to ask me.

'I'm telling her a lot of stories.'

'She doesn't hit so much anymore. I want to know how this happened!'

'I have no idea – ask her.'

'But that's why I'm calling. She said "I'm waiting until tomorrow!" and then she said, "Maybe God will give me a present if I wait."'

'She said that?'

'Yes. I told her, "I'm going to give you a lot of hugs" and she told me she wanted a different present. I said, "What?" She said she didn't know. I told her hugs were my favorite present.'

I was speechless. Little defiant Ruby was internalizing the meanings of the stories. I couldn't wait to see her.

Ruby once again opened the huge door.

As we walked up the stairs, I said, 'Ruby, I talked with your teacher. She told me you're not hitting your friends anymore.'

'I am, too.'

'You're still hitting your friends at school?'

'Yes. Mom says I am.'

'Are you still hitting your brother?'

'I don't know.'

Anna greeted me in an exhausted tone of voice. She looked thinner than ever. 'Yes, she is still hitting the baby – she still does whatever she wants.'

'May we talk when I am done playing with Ruby?'

She shrugged. 'I might be too busy with the baby, but if I'm not…okay.'

Ruby was pulling me into her room.

I was getting accustomed to Ruby's way of thinking. Often her thoughts were flighty and it was hard to follow what she was trying to express. Our recent conversation was typical, and often when I told her stories, her attention span was short, and she interrupted, imitating my tone of voice, expressing her thoughts fast and furious.

'This time I am going to tell you a story,' she said in her dramatic fashion. 'Now you have to sit down.' She pointed to a spot on the floor and I sat there. She rummaged through her bookshelf until she found an animal picture book. She sat down next to me and proceeded to 'read the story' by looking at the pictures.

I asked her if she would like me to write down what she was saying in order to make her own story. She agreed, at first with uncertainty. 'Are you writing *everything* I'm saying?' she asked.

'Yes, I am writing everything,' I said.

'Well, you have to write everything.'

'Ruby, continue to tell me about your story, so I can keep writing.'

This is the story Ruby told me, along with my story response.

The Lion, the Giraffe, and the Polar Bear

by Ruby Costava

One day in the forest the monkeys were having fun, climbing trees and eating bananas. There was a nice lion. He said, 'Hi,' to the other lions and to the monkeys. Then the giraffe became friends when everyone met. They sang together and slept over at each other's houses.

The polar bear was mean. He bit people, killed them in the water, and cut their brains. He cracked people in fire, and he said, 'Police, go into the fire there or I'll crack your body open, you monsters.'

The lion and the giraffe and the monkeys couldn't do anything. Then they had a plan. They wanted to throw him into the deep forest where all the wolves were. When the polar bear was deep in the forest, he screamed, 'AHHHHHHHH ...!' and he ate the wolves.

The moral is: Be careful of mean animals, because some animals are nice and some are mean.

They wanted to throw him into the deep forest where all the wolves were. The wolves that year had a great hunting season. They caught many animals, and their food pantries were stocked full. So when the polar bear was thrown at them, they were not interested. The polar bear screamed, 'AHHHHHH...!' and tried to eat the wolves. But the wolves thought the bear was singing. As the bear screamed, he jumped and danced around trying to snatch at the wolves, but when wolves are full they are kind. They looked curiously at the bear, and when he paused, they asked him, 'What kind of song and dance is this, Mr Bear, and why are you here with us, the wolves?'

The bear was so overcome with their politeness, he couldn't speak. He sat down on the forest floor and scratched his furry head. 'I'm the meanest there is,' he suddenly screamed. But this had no effect on the wolves. They knew that when they were hungry, they too could be uite mean. However, they were confident about themselves and didn't need to prove anything to the bear. 'Well, if you think so,' said the wolves, 'that's fine with us. Meantime, if you're hungry, come and have a bite to eat with us.'

Bewildered, the bear followed them into their cave and saw a beautiful feast set. He sniffed the air of delicious meat, and couldn't wait. Once he had eaten, he felt much better. 'Gee,' he said, 'Do you guys eat police or people, or crack fires?'

The wolves didn't know what he was talking about.

'Fires are nice in winter,' said one baby wolf. 'We love to be warm.'
'Yeah,' cried the community of wolves, 'Could you help us stay warm in the
winter?' The polar bear agreed. And because of his knowing how to stay
warm in the winter, he eventually was asked to go to the North Pole to help
all the poor shivering creatures up there. And that is why to this day the
polar bear lives at the North Pole, and he is happy as the wolves in their
den, and the monkeys climbing trees eating bananas.

The moral is: If you are feeling mean, find out where you are most
useful, and go help someone who could use your gifts.

When the story was finished, I said, 'Ruby, this is quite a story!'

'Well, only *this* part is finished.'

'This part, Ruby?' She nodded. 'When you go, I'm going to write some more and make a whole book.'

'I think that is great. How's about making a drawing for your book, while I think about my own ending to this story?'

She became upset. 'I want to draw a picture, but I *can't.* I don't know how to draw a lion or a giraffe.'

She picked up the animal book and looked at the pictures. She became more agitated. 'I don't know how to draw a giraffe like that.'

'Hey, it's okay, you monkey!' I said, but she wouldn't be distracted. 'Look, I don't know how to make a giraffe either.'

I showed Ruby how I would draw these animals, explaining to her that perfection was not important. I said, 'You see, this looks nothing like that giraffe in the picture. I didn't even try to draw it perfectly, but I drew it with joy. And that's what makes it fun.'

She watched me very carefully as I drew the animals. She picked up her crayon and copied what I did, but of course her animals turned out completely differently. As she drew, she said, 'Look at mine! I'm making my animals with lots of colors.' And she took great care to make her drawing as colorful as she could.

When your weakest aspects are challenged?

I am visually-spatially challenged. I could never 'draw properly' as a child, but when I was a student, studying social work, I took some art therapy classes which freed me from the need to 'draw perfectly.' I learned how to play with crayons, markers, acrylic, and watercolor. As I engaged in different mediums, I let go of my fears of 'not being able to draw.' To my surprise, when I met children who said they couldn't draw, my own issues around this felt healed enough for me both to identify with their problem, and to guide them. Drawing *with* children rather than watching, is a valuable way of showing them what is possible. I still can't draw, but I do know how to play and create and have fun. This is all a child needs to see in order to begin the visual art process.

While she drew, I came up with my story response.

She didn't like my story. 'I like mine better,' Ruby said, 'cause animals eat each other.'

'You know, Ruby, you are right. Animals do eat each other. I'm wondering if there are any bears in your life?'

'No.'

Both DSS and Anna had told me that Ruby's father was under investigation for suspected verbal and physical abuse of Ruby. The allegations had arisen during her recent visitations. Her story and her behavior certainly indicated that she had witnessed and experienced abusive incidents. It would probably be a while before she could talk about any of it. The story was a pretty good start.

'Well, anybody could be the bear – a friend, your brother.'

'My brother isn't a bear!'

'Okay, well then, you could be a bear!' I tickled her. 'Or your dad or your mom or your teacher…'

'Sometimes I hit my friends at school, and sometimes I hit my brother.'

'Thank you for telling me the truth Ruby, that was a really good job. Your teacher tells me though, you are doing better with your friends.'

'I still hit them.'

'What do you mean, Ruby?'

'I get mad at them.'

I was realizing that Ruby actually believed hitting and anger were the same thing. I wondered just how volatile her father was, how quick did his temper rise out of a calmness, and how violently did he explode? How often, in a day, in an hour, did this happen?

When it was time to go, Ruby followed me out and ran to her mother who was, once again, holding the baby. She showed her story and picture to Anna.

'I can't look at it now, I'm feeding your brother.'

'But I did it myself, you have to see my picture, you have to.'

Anna didn't say anything. Ruby sat down next to her, and tried to grab her brother. 'I want to play with him, you have to let me have him – give him to me so I can see his face.'

Anna turned away in order to feed him in peace. 'You are exhausting, Ruby. Please leave me alone until I am done.'

I looked at Ruby, who looked disappointed and contemplative.

'I'll tell you what,' I said, 'next session I'll bring the story all typed and you can read it out loud to Mom.'

The next day I went to see Anna alone. She greeted me kindly, her long thin hair untied and loose all around her thin long face, and bony shoulders.

'Hi,' she said. 'Come in. The baby is asleep.'

She seemed tense and hesitant in her speech, as though she was not sure how to handle me. It was as if she were asking herself, would I spill everything to DSS? Could I be trusted?

'I just want to know more about Ruby, about what her life was like when her father lived with you?'

Anna's entire body stiffened. 'He's gone. Why should I talk about him?'

When the client says 'No': Going further with an issue

When I confronted Anna about Ruby's father, I felt tension in the room and I didn't quite know what to do. I felt strongly that Anna needed to talk, but her defense was huge. Would I be emotionally intruding? Would I be re-enacting the perpetrator by forcing a vulnerability to come through? Would a vulnerability come out within me that I wouldn't be able to handle in the moment? I was quiet for a few seconds, sitting with my doubts and with Anna's defense. I realized in those few seconds that we were more or less feeling the same fear, for different reasons. I knew I was emotionally stronger than Anna, and that I could face my own fears as well as hold hers. Silently naming this helped me find my courage. I knew I could handle Anna's vulnerabilities safely as long as I was sensitive and asked her permission to proceed.

At a later time, when Anna refused to talk again, I began feeling 'rejected' by Anna, a strong reminder of my own history. Anna's own fears of rejection were present so the entire 'feel' of the room was nearly impossible for me to bear. I needed a few moments to sit with and face my feelings of fear, to overcome this perceived difficulty and to again have faith in the process. There was no reason to continue to push Anna more – if I stayed in touch with my own feelings as well as Anna's, the process would eventually shed more light on Anna's relationship to her ex. I decided on two actions: I would choose a more comfortable subject for both of us to talk about (Ruby), and I would tell Anna a story: Ruby's story.

'Hmm…he's hard to talk about?'

Anna shrugged. 'He's gone and there is no point in talking about him.'

'May I ask some more questions?'

'I don't see the point.'

'He is Ruby's father, and I understand she still sees him. And the more I know about him, the more I can help Ruby.'

'I'm sure DSS has told you everything.'

'No. I don't believe DSS knows much of anything except that he is the baby's father as well, and that you kicked him out because he was supposedly abusive.'

'He was.'

'Can you tell me what he did?'

'He yelled. He threw things. He was terrible to me.' Her body was stiffening to a point of rigidity.

'Anna, thank you for telling me. I am so sorry this happened to you. Anna, can I tell you something about Ruby?'

'What?'

'I really like her. I think she is creative and really smart.'

Anna shrugged.

'Do you know that her teacher called to tell me that she has stopped hitting?'

'Yes, she called me too. That teacher should come live here. Ruby hasn't changed at all.'

'So you haven't seen any changes?'

'No.'

'Are you glad that her teacher is?'

'Why can't Ruby change for *me*? Can't she see how tired I am? You have no idea how tiring a child she is.'

The amount of validation and caretaking Anna needed was extensive. All the while she was talking with me, she spoke in a flat tone. Both DSS and I agreed she was depressed, and in need of her own psychiatric care. Anna was adamant that she didn't need 'that kind of help.'

'Look, I brought along a story Ruby has written, and the picture she drew to go with it. I also wrote a story in response to hers. May I read it to you?'

I read the story out loud to her, and a smile actually lifted the corners of her mouth.

'It's like Ruby to write such a violent story.'

'How so?'

'I'm afraid she is like her father.'

'How so?'

'He is very demanding. And he is angry and controlling. He said things like, "You have to do this now." But he became very angry if I didn't listen in that moment.'

'I am so sorry this happened to you. It must have taken some strength to leave him.'

'I had to. The last time he got mad, I was pregnant. I banged my head and went unconscious; he got scared and called 911. That's what he tells me. I know he pushed me hard, and that's how I banged my head. But you know, the cops knew about him and took him to jail as the ambulance took me to the hospital. DSS was called again. He had to go.'

'Oh, I am so sorry and so glad you have not taken him back.'

'I do miss him sometimes. He wasn't always like that.'

'No?'

'No, he could be fun, you know. He was from Puerto Rico, he had that Latino way. He could be fun.' Her smile very gently returned. 'He wasn't all bad, you know?'

I did know.

'Thank you for taking the time today. I think I can help Ruby better now. I can't promise that I can make her change, but I can help her more clearly now. Oh, just one other thing: when you feel that Ruby is acting like her father, you can try saying to yourself, while Ruby is acting like her father, she is not her father...and that will help you see Ruby as Ruby.' But Anna had withdrawn. She was back in her own world. Even this little exercise in reality testing was too much for her.

I took my leave, amazed even so, at the effects of Ruby's story on Anna.

We can't escape telling stories

Our lives are filled with storytelling, not only outwardly, but also inside ourselves. We really do tell stories all of the time. We also re-create them as time goes by. The stories Anna was telling herself about her own reality were increasing ten-fold with the repeat of them in her mind. Trying to ease someone out of their own story experience was difficult. It was breaking a deep-seated belief system. I was realizing that telling stories was acting like a homeopathic remedy. I was treating the malady with malady itself.

Treating story with story, as a means of thinking differently, as a means of choosing another view from which to see yourself and those you love, is another reason why stories are so healing!

Roberto continued to have trouble listening to his teachers, and Maria was crying often, particularly in her sleep, and on waking up.

I worked with them around their beliefs about crying, telling them that crying was a necessary human need. I tried to help them create a relationship to their pain.

Helping children create a relationship to their pain

Suffering is an innate part of life, and bad things happen all of the time, *beginning* in childhood. We as parents and caretakers often believe that children should always be happy. However, this puts an enormous burden on children, as well as ourselves. Children, like parents, experience myriad sadnesses on a daily basis And children are constantly reminding us of our own pain, bringing out all of our inadequacies, because we are inadequate at facing our own pain. We don't want to revisit our childhood/adolescent crises. Instinctively, we want to push it all away, and we especially do not want our children to suffer in the way we have.

However, think about the times you cried and suffered the most, and think about what those times of darkness taught you. One of the very best gifts we can give our children is permission to suffer. As the parents or caretakers, we can guide children through their dark times. The more we face our own pain, the more we help our children face theirs. In so doing, a genuine strength and courage is created, and this inner strength, taught in childhood, is a strength which no suffering can ever weaken or take away. It is a strength that allows empathy, courage, humor, and health to thrive.

If Roberto and Maria could make a relationship to their pain of abandonment, then they would be creating an unbreakable, honest strength that would help them face suffering throughout their lives. With this self-awareness, they might enter into a healthy life-style as teenagers and then adults, without having to repeat/act out the issues of abandonment over and over, even though the pain of the abandonment may never disappear. Stories, of course, are one great way to create such a relationship.

At their house, as they drew, I said to Roberto and Maria, 'Look, what did Adam and Eve do when that gate swung closed behind them?'

'They cried.'

'Right. And did the crying make them feel better or worse?'

'Better!' Roberto and Maria answered each question in unison, and they jumped up and down each time they noticed that they spoke at the same time.

'That's right. And why did they feel better?'

"Cause they knew crying was a present!' Maria said.

"Cause they knew crying ummm, ummm, ummm, was a present from God!' Roberto cried, jumping up and landing all over Maria. They were rolling around each other, giggling.

'That's right,' I said, laughing. Their joy was contagious.

I asked both of them to come sit in front of me. They were laughing uncontrollably. They sat in front of me, and for a few minutes I asked them to take a deep breath, and then I asked them to place their hands in my opened palms. 'This is great. It is quiet and calm. Take another deep breath.'

They did.

'Maria, when you cry every night and in the morning…'

'I don't know why.'

'I know. That's okay. Are you feeling sad or happy when you cry?'

'Sad.'

'Like Adam and Eve?'

Her eyes lit up.

'Yeah! Just like them! Crying is a present from God!'

'Well…yes…,' I said hesitantly. 'That's what the story says, that crying is a present from God. Maybe the feeling of sadness is also a present from God.'

Roberto was jumping up and down again and saying excitedly, 'YES, YES, YES!!!!! Grandma says everything comes from God, so even sadness and even yelling and not listening comes from God!'

And he pulled Maria up, and now they were dancing up and down screaming 'YES' at the top of their lungs.

Had I introduced a monster or a solution? I felt that contagious joy catch inside me. These children were delightful, and that delight came up no matter what, no matter how sad or defiant they were. I had to remind myself what they had experienced, and the level of abandonment they had lived through in their so short lives. I also realized that they were creating a new relationship to their pain!

Mrs Cruz walked into the room, hands on hips, waiting to reprimand. But she was soon laughing along too. She sent them to the kitchen, ordering them to eat, asking me if I would eat as well.

When I declined she shook her head.

'You don't eat, Molly?'

'Of course I do!' I was shocked by the question. Eating is one of my favorite pastimes!

Breaking therapeutic boundaries

When Mrs Cruz invited me to eat, I was actually quite hungry, but those issues about boundaries and clients were coming up again. These included: 'Do not socialize or barter with your clients; do not cry in front of your clients; do not ask your clients for anything, food, help, etc.' These rules were deeply engrained in me. However, home-based therapy in itself was already breaking one of those rules. By virtue of simply being in my client's home, the therapy itself was far more personal than in an office. My clients were natural hosts, and they often felt insulted if I refused their generosity. For their generosity, most of the time, was a gesture straight from their hearts.

Understanding when and how to break these rules, and when and how to keep them, was a process. Mrs Cruz was so totally sincere, that she did not see the client-therapist boundary like I did. I was a visitor in her home helping her with her grandchildren, and offering me food was the most natural thing for her to do. She would have not understood the concept of 'client-therapist boundary' in this way. Because of her sincerity, I accepted her offering, and surprising things came of it.

'You are too thin. I don't think you eat. Come, have a small plate.'

It was useless to protest.

Soon she came out with a tomato-colored mixture on top of a huge plate of rice. It smelled great. Chicken, beans, hot peppers, chili powder, garlic, onions, green peppers – the taste was exquisite. The heat of the food, the flavor and the texture went all the way down through my bones as if I hadn't eaten for a long time. Grandma's cooking. I had forgotten what it tasted like.

Mrs Cruz derived great pleasure from watching me eat. Her eyes followed my fork down to my plate, and then up to my mouth. Her face broke out into broad smiles while she nodded with approval. It was as if she had found a starving animal and was now bringing it back to life.

I realized then how the children felt being in her care. I put myself in their shoes and felt what it must have been like for them. I stiffened up my own feelings and remembered the pain of abandonment. I felt sadness immediately, and then huge amounts of rage heated up in my body. Now I knew why Maria cried and Roberto yelled.

Then I put myself in their place, entering Mrs Cruz's care. I felt her true love, her delicious food which contained her love, and her genuine pleasure in watching all of this disparity find its joy. More sadness and anger arose. It was safe now to have these feelings. It was safe now to tap into innate and true joy.

Mrs Cruz and I looked at each other. 'I don't think you quite know what you are doing for these children, they are so lucky to have you,' I said.

'I don't know. There was no choice; when the DSS called, I just came, anybody would. My son, he was hard, you know? I was so young. Just 18. My husband, he was no good. Too much alcohol, you know?' She took a deep breath. 'He leave, he go to Miami and then here to Boston. My son very sad and very hard to be with. When he was 16 he left to find his father.' She sighed. Her round black eyes were thoughtful, outlining the wrinkles surrounding her forehead. 'I tried. You know. And I was very sad in Dominican, but I have my daughter there. She is a good girl, you know? She is happy I am bringing Roberto and Maria home, they will have cousins there. And I have a very beautiful garden. You will have to come visit.' She beamed again, looking so much like Maria I had to keep searching her face to remind myself who she was.

I felt incredible warmth coming from her. I didn't have to tell her about Roberto's and Maria's innate joy. She already knew about it, and told me stories about them. For example, she told me that even though Roberto still yelled at the teacher, he was also calming down. She told me how Maria and he had found some wild flowers and came home surprising her with them. She couldn't tell who was more pleased, the children or she. She told me that, a few mornings ago, Maria had been crying in her bed. When she walked in to comfort her, Roberto was there. He was asking her, 'Who do you miss more, Mom or Dad? Because I miss them, only how can I miss Mom when I didn't even know her?'

I asked her, 'So when you find Maria crying in the morning, what do you do?'

'Oh, I tell her, shhhhhhhh, do not cry. It is okay. I tell her about the Dominican and about my garden and how big the fruits are, and she laughs! But she did say something strange. She said, "If I cry there, then we can stay, because Adam and Eve left their garden and then they cried after." I told her she could stay forever, and that I was in charge, and that God said, "Go ahead, Grandma Cruz, be in charge!"'

Sometimes it's enough to sit and listen

I considered whether to tell Mrs Cruz the story of Adam and Eve or not. I decided against it; she had already changed the story for Maria, and the telling of the story once again would have acted like a defense for me. It would have been avoiding the story that Mrs Cruz was telling me, and the genuine profundity it was bringing to me.

Sometimes, it is just enough to sit and listen. I was discovering a deeper importance to keeping quiet after I tell a story. To explain or talk, really counteracts the healing ingredients of a story, and the major ingredient is listening even after the story is told.

Note

1   Adapted from *Keepers of the Night: Native American Stories and Nocturnal Activities for Children* by Michael J. Caduto and Joseph Bruchac (1994) Golden, CO: Fulcrum Publishing. Used with permission from Fulcrum Publishing.

CHAPTER TWELVE

Exploring New Constellations

It was an unusually beautiful day for August. The sky clear, the air dry.

I had been working with Nancy steadily since that family meeting at the YMCA. Lynn had recovered from her relapse and she was struggling hard. DSS had found group therapy for both Nancy and Linda and this was helping Nancy understand herself better and not feel so alone. Lynn was still expecting way too much from Nancy, and was still involved with Kevin. He was like a secret; they didn't want anyone to know they were still seeing each other.

Six weeks into third grade, six months after meeting her, Nancy was excelling in school. She proved to be highly imaginative, argumentative, and generous. She had stopped getting into trouble at school, and even Lynn acknowledged she was listening better.

Nancy had heard several stories from me, and we were working with them constantly. The one which stuck in her mind, though, was the *The Creation Story*. She was very curious about God.

'Is that story true? I mean did He really give us crying? If He gave us crying because we don't listen, why doesn't he give everybody in the whole world food? Does He make people starve if they don't listen too?'

I had no answer.

'Nancy, these are great questions. Sometimes it takes many years to find the answers to questions like these. So I want to encourage you to keep asking these questions to anyone you wish.'

'But is it *true*?'

The truth in stories

When children ask questions about the truth of stories, they are not looking for the literal truth of the events. They are asking themselves about moral behavior, about the merits of right and wrong. Nancy needed to continue to explore this question, not to have it answered. It reminded me of a poem I wrote for my daughter, a few years earlier, when she turned 12:

For Sarah Age 12

Two crescent moons curve your hips
rose petals line your breasts
the Goddess has placed stardust in your eyes
and carved your cheeks with Her kiss

Your body is preparing for starling flight
as your mind lifts and opens
it will fall into caves and unknown crevices

Black and hard
back against rock
your face pressed into moldy air

There is no protection here
only my love will guide from on top
and the Goddess will ride your memory

In the casement of your growth
in the grief I cannot hold you from
the Goddess is planting questions
which you must become

'What do you think?' I replied. 'Is it true?'

'I don't know. I don't get why some people have money, and other people don't.'

'That's also a truly wonderful question, Nancy, and I'm wondering if you would like to explore this more through writing your own story?'

She set to work with zeal, becoming more and more excited as she watched her own story deepen.

'Why is the bad guy, Mr Anderson, bad?'

'I don't know.'

'What "bad" sort of things does he do?

'He steals…I know! He's going to steal Mrs Tina's ring!'

'Why does he want that ring?'

'He wants a lot of money…I know! He isn't really poor or anything and he isn't really rich, he's right in the middle, and maybe he joined a gang, but his family doesn't know…I know! He wants to steal, he doesn't want to work!'

Not only did Nancy engage in the telling of the story with great enthusiasm and amazing seriousness, but she also worked painstakingly hard at her illustrations. When she was creating the couch in the first illustration, she couldn't decide whether to color it brown or pink. She experimented on a separate piece of paper, coloring the couch one color and then the other. Finally, Nancy put the two colors together, and cried excitedly, 'Look, a tweed couch!' She shook back her curly brown hair and looked at me with her great blue eyes. 'Do we have time for me to finish the picture?'

'Yes. Can you listen to my ending of the story while you color?'

She nodded, her head bent close to the paper.

Mr and Mrs Tina

by Nancy Rizzo

Five years ago in a town, a rich woman named Mrs Tina was celebrating her 28th birthday. She got a lot of gifts from Mr Tina. Her favorite gift was a 14 karat gold ring. She put it in a safe place, and a bad guy named Mr Anderson saw her put it in the safe. He went into the house and stole the ring.

Figure 10. 'Mr and Mrs Tina' by Nancy Rizzo

Figure 11. 'Mr and Mrs Tina' by Nancy Rizzo

Mrs Tina went to the dining room to eat. The next day Mrs Tina asked Mr Tina to go get her 14 karat gold ring. When he opened the safe, he screamed. Mrs Tina said, 'What's wrong?' Mr Tina said, 'Your 14 karat gold ring I bought you is gone!'

So they both called the police. When the policemen came, they said, 'What happened?' Mr Tina said, 'Someone stole the 14 karat gold ring I gave Mrs Tina.' The cops said, 'We have a bunch of guns to hunt this person down.' But Mr Tina said, 'You don't need a bunch of guns and stuff, we have a crystal ball you can look into to find where he or she is.'

The police said, 'Okay, let's use it.' So they used it and they tracked down where Mr Anderson was. Mr Anderson wasn't rich or poor. He lived in the middle, but he was part of a gang. He stole lots of stuff but the ring was the most valuable he had. He stole because he wanted a lot of money for his family, but his family didn't know he belonged to a gang.

The cops had a long journey to where he was. When they got there, they immediately went to see where he was, and they said, 'Freeze, or we will shoot you.'

So the cops pretended they had real guns, but they were fake guns. So Mr Anderson freezed, and they handcuffed him and sent him to prison.

So Mrs Tina got her ring back and had several children and loved them all.

The moral is: You shouldn't leave your windows open so someone can see what you are doing.

They said, 'Freeze, or we will shoot you.' Mr Anderson tried to run, but the cops grabbed him, kicked him, and threw him to the ground. They arrested him and sent him to prison. However, it was too late for Mrs Tina. The ring had been sold, and no one knew where it was. Mrs Tina was sad at the loss of her ring. However, she had many children, and she loved them all. Her children taught her that the love and imagination which come from the heart were far more important than the value of her stolen ring.

The moral of the story is: Things of value can be stolen and never returned, but imagination and love will always be safe within the hearts of those who value them.

Nancy did not like my ending at all.

'You have too much violence. The cops should never hit anybody. No one should ever hit anybody.'

She said she wanted to be a lawyer when she grew up, 'Because lawyers make a lot of money, and then I can help all of the poor people not be poor again. I will argue for them, and give them things.'

'Nancy, thank you for telling me this story. You are very thoughtful.'

'That's what my teacher says too. I asked her what that means, and she said "Full of thoughts. Full of nice thoughts." I do think a lot. I'm not nice to my mother sometimes. But she's not nice to me. I hate that.'

'I know what you mean. Sometimes it's hard to not fight, and Mr Anderson and Mrs Tina, they are all there right inside of you. You can choose who you wish to imitate, but you can't choose until you know who is talking inside of you.'

A big risk. Would she understand?

'You mean, if I am mean, I am Mr Anderson and if I am nice, I am Mrs Tina?'

'Yeah! When you don't want to listen to Mom, and you argue and you know you are acting like Mr. Anderson, then you can say, "I am acting like Mr Anderson," and then you can choose to act like Mrs Tina. You can say, "What would Mrs Tina do right now?"'

'She would look into her crystal ball to see what to do!'

'And what is your crystal ball?'

'Trying to help everybody.'

I didn't see Nancy again. They were consistently not home for their appointments, and finally Lynn called to tell me she was doing too much, but would let me know when she could make steady appointments again. I couldn't really tell from our conversation how things were going. Lynn did tell me though that Nancy was calming down, and Linda was becoming the greater problem. Linda was now expressing her anger in a way she couldn't before. Now that Nancy was shouting less she was giving Linda room to shout out her anger. I explained this to Lynn on the phone. We ended up talking for an hour, an entire session.

'So when Linda calms down, Nancy will start again?'

'Not necessarily, not if you give Linda a chance to tell you she's angry. I mean, think about it Lynn, she has a lot to be mad about.'

'But I'm doing better, her father's better, we're not fighting when he is here, just arguing. What does she have to be mad about?'

We continued to talk. I'm not sure Lynn quite understood. Eventually, she said, 'You know that story Nancy wrote? Well, Nancy is reading it to Linda. She keeps asking Linda "Who do you want to be like, Mrs Tina or Mr Anderson?"'

When we said goodbye, I pictured Nancy helping Linda. She sure was using her 'crystal ball.' The power of story was helping Nancy pull on her own inner creativity, a strength that had always been there.

I had met Ruby at her school a few times. Each time she was very happy to see me. She often ordered me to watch while she flew down the slide, or rode a scooter. She did have trouble relating to her peers, and with her teachers' help, she was slowly understanding the difference between ordering someone about and making a request.

On this particular day, I was at Ruby's home. When we settled in her room, she immediately said, 'Everyone at school is mean to me. No one does what I say, and I always get in trouble, and I don't do anything.'

'Mmmmmmmm…you don't do *anything*?'

She shook her head.

'Mmmmmmmmmm…' I had her previous story with me. I read it once more to her. 'Who are the monkeys and lions in your class and who is the mean polar bear?'

Ruby squinted her eyes. 'I don't know. My mom says I'm like the witch in *Snow White* sometimes – do you know that movie?' Before I could respond, she said, 'I know! Maybe I could make another story!'

She had no problem making up the characters, and like a true artist she abandoned her original thoughts the minute she began to tell the story. She loved both my story response and her story. In hearing my ending, she hopped around like a frog, ribbiting and having a wonderful time.

Untitled

by Ruby Costava

Once upon a time, there was a girl named Lisa. She lived in a big blue house. And she moved away into a big red pink blue green rainbow colorful house. And she went to school one day and she found a friend named Ruby. Then we tickled each other during story time.

Something happened. We got in trouble for not listening to the story. Then we had to go down to Mrs Connor's room. It was boring. We had to stay for the whole day until five days. We tried to escape. We tried going out the window but the windows were closed. They were locked. But the door was open, so we sneaked on our tippy toes and we made it. Then we got our hats and backpacks. Then we ate our snack.

Then we left. Then I went to my house, and she went to her house. But then I watched some TV. Then in a little while I asked my mom if I could go to my friend's house. She was in her backyard. I went in her backyard, and she was there playing on the swing upside down on the bars. Hanging there so high I couldn't even reach. The rainbow house is haunted. There was a mean old witch living in it. She ran after us after we went inside. Then we tried to escape but she caught us. And she made us out of soup. Actually, she turned us into a chicken. We bited her with our chicken mouth.

There was a prince that came to kiss us when we was a chicken. He thought that there were two Snow Whites. But there wasn't. Then when we turned back, we said, 'Why did you kiss when we was a chicken?' The witch turned us into chicken instead of a big huge mountain. She did the whole thing wrong!

The witch still was alive, but she didn't catch us again. Lisa moved with me in my house with some of her toys. The prince liked us, and he killed the witch for us.

The moral is: Do not go into a house if it's haunted. You have to check there is no spiders or spider webs or witch stuff or a witch.

The prince cried, 'I really thought I would have two Snow Whites, or at least a Sleeping Beauty and a Snow White. And what do you mean, the witch did everything wrong? Thank goodness you weren't turned into a big huge mountain. Then I would have climbed you, not kissed you!' But the witch was after us, so Lisa and I ran as fast as we could back to our house.

Thank goodness she remembered to bring some toys. 'I hope that prince is alright,' Lisa said, breathing hard.

'Me too. Do you think we should go back there?'

'Not on your life.'

'But maybe the prince needs some help. I KNOW!! Let's grab a net. Come on,' I said, grabbing Lisa with one hand and my net with the other.

We ran back to that big colorful rainbow house. We heard terrible screams in the yard. The prince was trying to kill the witch.

'Watch this,' I whispered to Lisa. I swung my net round and round just like my mom had taught me, and when it was ready it made a perfect swirl right over the witch's head, and landed on top of her. She was caught! Lisa and I jumped with excitement, and the prince looked bewildered when we appeared before him.

'Hhhhhhoooow…whhhhhaaaatttt…'

'You silly prince,' I said, 'I was just trying to help you. My teacher says this is teamwork. You cornered the witch, and I caught her! I put out my hand and shook his. 'Good work!' I said, and we all grinned. But the witch was moaning, and turning all kinds of colors, and suddenly there were millions of frogs hopping and leaping all over Lisa's yard. The witch was nowhere to be seen. Since frogs are too hard to catch, and anyway are pretty harmless, except for their warts, we left them alone. On the way back to my house, the prince laughed out loud.

'What's so funny?' Lisa and I asked at the same time.

'I used to be one of those frogs!'

The moral of the story is: Listen to your parents and teachers — sometimes they may have useful and wise things to teach you.

'Is school boring?'

'Yes… Hey, how did you know school is boring?'

'Well, it says so right here in your story!'

'Oh yeah! I hate going in time out, and I go all the time.'

'Yeah? You alone, or you and a friend?'

'My friend never listens.'

'In your story she did. The two of you helped each other, remember?'

'Oh yeah!' Ruby said this laughing. 'Hey, I know! Maybe we could help each other tomorrow!'

'How?'

'I don't know but, hey, I know! Let's make a picture to my story. Maybe I could show it to her!' And she drew and talked the rest of the session, the story processing deep within, allowing more creativity and more choices to develop.

As the session was ending, I asked Ruby if she would sit with me while I showed her mother the stories. Ruby held my hand as she skipped into the kitchen.

Anna read Ruby's stories out loud.

'Well,' replied her mother, 'Molly's right in her story about the polar bear, 'cause he becomes nice. You know, you don't always have to be mean. Sometimes you can be nice. I'll keep this story for you so you won't lose it.'

'Uh-uh! No sir!' protested Ruby. 'My story is way better 'cause... 'cause ...'cause bears are mean and they eat wolves. That's what has to happen. It has to.'

Anna was silent, resigned.

'Let her know she's done a good job,' I whispered to Anna.

'Ruby, those are good stories. I like your pictures. Your teacher called. She said you were doin' better too. Now all you have to do is do better here with me.'

Ruby snuggled close to Anna. The baby was sleeping and Anna's arms were free. She put them around Ruby. 'Will you listen to me now, Ruby?'

Ruby was quiet, I'd never seen her this quiet. She climbed into her mother's lap, and lay her face against her mother's shoulders. Anna put her arms lightly around Ruby. She closed her eyes.

I took my leave, looking at them one more time. I couldn't tell who was smaller, who was needier. It didn't matter, something was already changing.

The bear was lying down with the wolf. Just like my version of Ruby's story indicated.

Facing the monster and living to tell about it

Writing stories, telling life stories and becoming more self-aware; this is the greatest story of all. The more you can face reality in your life, the less stressful your life becomes, less even though the stressful events still exist. Ruby's first story, so violent, deeply expressed both her conscious and unconscious understanding of reality. By writing this in an imaginative form, and by reading it out loud to her mother, whom she loved most in the world, she had her experiences validated, even if they were not directly expressed. Through this validation, Ruby had a chance to face her demanding nature, and a chance to learn how to make friends differently. It was impossible for her to do this before her story writing because the monster-part of her life was controlling her, rather than vice versa.

It is a tremendous paradox, that the more you face the monster, the less hold he has on both your inner and outer world. Once you've faced reality, the healing process can then weave through your life, on deeper and deeper levels. You really don't have to go anywhere to find this process. It is not magical, as so many of my clients had taught me. It is about the nitty-gritty process of facing suffering, and having courage.

That same day I received a call from DSS. Anna, the baby, and Ruby had moved without giving a new address. As yet, no one knew where they were. Why did Anna pick up and leave like that? What was going on in her mind? I remembered how I left them and how hard it is to break out of the victim role. If it is embedded within you long enough, and for enough generations, it becomes so deep a belief system as to become almost like a religion. Was Anna totally and completely unprepared for change? Would Ruby have the encouragement to continue in her process? I would never know the answers. I never saw Ruby or Anna again.

'Remember that story about crying?' Maria asked.

'Yes!'

'Maria cried and said she missed Mom, and then I cried.'

'And then Grandma hugged us!' Maria jumped up again.

'Would you like to write your own story?'

'YES!' they cried in unison.

'Who is going to be the good character?'

'A little girl,' shouted Maria.

'No, a little boy,' shouted Roberto.

'Hmmm, a little girl, a little boy – which will it be?'

'BOTH' cried Maria.

'Yeah, both,' echoed Roberto.

'Okay! One can be the good character, and the other can be the helping friend.'

'Yeah!'

'So who is going to be the bad character?'

'A man!'

'Yeah! Tyron!' cried Maria.

'Yeah! Tyron! No, David!'

'No! Tyron.'

'Okay, Tyron.'

'Alright, gee, I really like the way you guys are figuring this all out. Let's see, do you want a magical object?'

'What do you mean?' asked Maria.

'Yes, a magic feather!' cried Roberto.

'A magic feather?'

'No, no, I mean a magic stone.'

'No! A magic crystal!' shouted Maria.

'Yes! A magic crystal!' Roberto jumped up and down.

'Okay, and where does this story take place?'

'Take place?' they both asked.

'Mmmmm...like in the city, in the forest, on the beach.'

'In the forest!' they said both at once.

'When did this take place?'

'Huh?'

'Well...you see, when you write a story you have to have a time and a place. So you can say "yesterday" or "a long time ago" or "five years ago in the forest such and such a thing happened."'

'Five thousand years ago!' interrupted Roberto, jumping up again.

'No...like, aaaaaa, yesterday...or ummmm, how's about three days ago?'

'Three years ago!'

Once they started to tell the story, they did not need much help from me. As Roberto and Maria engaged in the telling of it, they practically acted it out.

Figure 12. 'The Magic Crystal' by Roberto Cruz

The Magic Crystal

by Roberto and Maria Cruz

Figure 13. 'The Magic Crystal' by Maria Cruz

Once upon a time three years ago in the woods, there lived a mean man named Tyron. Tyron was always yelling. He was very bossy. He never shared anything and he didn't have any friends.

The little girl Susie, and the little boy David, were friends and they also lived in the forest. They were good friends. They cared about people and they were looking for a little magic crystal.

They wanted to help the poor people and give them food. Tyron had stolen all of their food and things. The people of the forest had nothing. This crystal could make things real. The crystal could make food appear.

Both Tyron and the kids were looking for this crystal. The kids made a trap for Tyron. When he fell into the trap, the kids found the crystal at the edge of the cave. They helped all the people and gave Tyron one more chance to be good. He agreed to accept the chance and he did everything Susie and David told him to do. The cave turned to gold and grew magic crystals forever. Tyron became so good that he was given the title, 'Guardian of the Cave.' And he has been guarding the cave ever since.

They helped all the people and gave Tyron one more chance to be good. But he didn't want to be good. When the cave turned to gold he ran toward the cave and tried to pull out as many crystals as he could. But because he was so mean, and because his fingers were dirty with greed, the gold crystals turned Tyron to stone. You can always find the cave now, by the ugly stone statue that stands near it. It is a reminder that only those pure of heart can enter the magic cave.

I changed the ending to this story because I wanted to help Maria and Roberto understand what happens when you don't change. While they had a direct understanding of this from living with their father, I wanted two opposite viewpoints in front of them, so they would always have power to choose how they wanted to behave.

'Is there any ending you like better?'

'Mine, sort of,' Maria said.

'Why?'

'It's ugly,' chimed in Roberto.

'My ending is ugly?'

'Tyron is ugly.'

'Tyron is ugly in my ending?'

'Yes!' they shouted at once.

'And you don't like Tyron being ugly?'

'No! It's better when he's nice. I want to show this to Grandma and to all of my teachers.'

'Yeah!' Maria agreed.

They called their grandma into the room.

Mrs Cruz appeared, smelling of garlic and onions. 'What, what?'

They asked me to read the story while they drew pictures. I translated the story into Spanish as best as I could. Mrs Cruz had a huge smile.

'Do you know Roberto doesn't yell anymore at his teacher? Do you know he asks her if he can draw or write a story? He is so good. He got "very good" on his report card from school and Maria here, she said "I don't want to cry in the morning anymore" and she doesn't. Ay, Dios, they are such good children.'

'They always have been, eh, Señora?'

'Gracias a Dios. Siempre.'

I said goodbye and walked to my car, only to find that the windshield had been smashed to pieces, and my briefcase was missing. I ran back into the Cruz's home. I was visibly upset and shaking. I called the office to report this, and then I called a glass place which specialized in replacing windshields for cars. It was 6pm.

'Ay, Dios!' Mrs Cruz shook her head. 'They wanted drugs. They steal for anything. Ay, Molly, come in, eat. I am so sorry.'

Maria and Roberto were holding my hands. 'You can sleep over if you want!'

'Are you crying, Molly?' This from Roberto.

'Sort of.'

I was trying to hold onto my professional stance. There was something about this violation that was making me shake uncontrollably.

Maria patted my shoulder. 'Remember that story, Molly? Remember that crying is a present?' I nodded and smiled at Maria. She came and gave me a hug.

That was it. I excused myself and ran to the bathroom and sobbed. By the time I had refreshed myself, a plate of food was waiting for me, and the people had arrived to fix my car.

As I drove home, I suddenly understood how Roberto and Maria and Anna and Ruby felt hearing stories. If you don't have the ego-strength to hold the compassion that stories bring, they are too much to take in. The violation I had experienced, along with Maria's genuine compassion, touched on an enormous vulnerability I hardly had the strength to contain. I cried all the way home, understanding profoundly what I had received from Maria and Roberto. They enacted my own behavior toward them, while embodying and acting from the very essence of the story I told them. They gave to me their complete experience of compassion.

Three months later, Mrs Cruz signed the adoption papers. I was over at their house for the last time. They each had a copy of *The Magic Crystal*. We had cake and juice and Maria and Roberto told me stories of Grandma's house in the Dominican. I hugged each of them goodbye, and Mrs Cruz hugged me the longest. 'You come to Dominican. You have a home there now.'

As I drove away, my mind was filled with all the clients I had lost that month. Each child came into my mind, and I relived some of our sessions. Is this how Adam and Eve felt when that gate slammed behind them? Was I comparing my relationship to these families to the Garden of Eden? I suppose I was. Gardens come wild with unexpected finds. Each one of my clients was like that: a rare wild flower trying to find its way to the sun.

PART FOUR

The Butterfly

CHAPTER THIRTEEN

The Lone Stars

It was an unusually hot day for mid-June in 1998. Hurricanes were pounding the Dominican and the coast of Florida. As a result, this particular day was more humid than the rainforest. Everything was matted and sticking to itself.

The weather did not deter Rosa Veracruz who focused her intense energy on her family and on her eight-year-old son, Saul. Rosa's complaints about Saul were the same as the ones Maria and Clara had about their sons. (See Parts 1 and 2.) Saul was talking back to both the teachers, and to her, and was in general acting angry. The doctor had told Rosa that he thought Saul had ADHD. But she didn't believe him, and even if Saul did have ADHD, she didn't want to put him on 'no pills.'

Rosa was a small, robust woman with soft brown eyes, and a wide earthy face. She was the matriarch of matriarchs: a foster mother, a prominent church member, and a mother of two. She did not speak English, although she could understand it. Between my Spanish and her English, we managed to communicate pretty well. Saul spoke Spanish and English fluently.

Rosa's home was immaculate. Her kitchen was completely taken up by an oblong kitchen table that was covered by a white, plastic tablecloth with a red-pink floral print. Two long benches lined the table. Smells of sizzling garlic, onions, and peppers seeped from every corner. Chicken or pork was often frying with the garlic, and a pot of yellow rice sat on the stove, as inviting as a full moon.

She led me into the living room where pitch-black couches covered with soft black pillows lined two walls. The hardwood floor was uncovered, and a large gleaming glass coffee table, in the middle of the room divided the two sofas. Near the entrance hall was a huge box of toys and a playpen.

She was holding a baby in one hand, and the other three foster children, aged three to five, were playing together in the adjacent room with her seven-year-old daughter.

Her husband, Saul's father, was active in his childrens' lives. He was a tall, soft-spoken man who was interested in God and the work ethic. Hurricanes had demolished his community in the Dominican Republic that summer. He was gone for two months helping to rebuild the towns there. He was very worried about the present weather conditions.

Because his parents were so active in the community, Saul was well aware of the tragedies that had befallen many of his neighbors. He heard about the mother down the street who was shot by her boyfriend early one morning while walking her three school-aged children to school. He knew about the drug raid three blocks away and, because his mother took care of several foster children at a time, he understood that these youngsters were living with his family because their parents 'were not home and there was no food in the house.'

Rosa asked me to see Saul 'because he never listens to me. Not only that, I am getting notes and phone calls from the school that he jumps from his seat, calls out of turn, and does not listen to his teacher. I don't know what happened. He is such a good boy.' He was receiving these reports in spite of his numerous academic achievements. Saul excelled in school and had won 'artist of the month' three times in a row. These achievements were not as important to Rosa as his behavior. 'If he doesn't have respect, he will get nowhere. He embarrasses me and his family, and I don't understand – he used to be such a good boy.'

Saul reminded me of Clara's son, Ricardo. He began each of our sessions by jumping on one of the sofas, losing himself among the cushions. He had the hardest time sitting still. It took a good 15 minutes for him to settle, to draw, and to listen. Everything about him was lanky. His hands, fingers, feet, and toes. His charming smile was as wide as his nose was long. His shaved head made his round, dark eyes look bigger.

The only way I could get Saul's attention was by telling him stories. Once the story began, he settled, picked up the crayons and drew. He made very intricate drawings of all kinds of things.

I told him the following story, which I read out loud.

The Butterfly[1]

by Brother Blue

Once upon a time ago.

Bop-i-dee, bop-i-dee, bip, bopping, doo-wopping, a finger pop, a dat-tee-bop, a loo-way. A hop.

Ring around the rosi, tomorrow, now ago. Far away, cross the deep blue sea. No place away, right here away.

There was a little caterpillar. He was crawling around on the ground. He was crying.

Poor caterpillar. He had never seen a butterfly.

He didn't know what he was gonna be.

But he wanted to fly.

He said (scream on harmonica).

People thought he was saying Chicago blues.

But he never heard of Chicago. He was just paying dues like you and me.

There's something he wants to do. There's something he wants to be.

He had never seen a butterfly.

Poor orphan, no mother, no father, no brother, no sister.

A poor little caterpillar crawling around.

He made a crying sound (harmonica cry).

He didn't know, he didn't know, he didn't know what he was gonna be.

He had that yearning.

He wanted to boogie up to that sky.

He wanted to breakdance across the stars. To the sound of groovy guitars.

Because he heard those guitars, you know, in heaven.

This caterpillar, who had never seen a butterfly, looked up in the sky.

Guess what he saw?

Butterfly. He didn't know what to say. He went: ahhhhhhhhhh!

It was so beautiful, so wonderful, it was so magicky. It was so
  musicy, It was: so ahhhhhhhh, ahhhhhhh, ahhhhhhh.

Then he thought of something. Guess what he said?

'I could dig it! I could dig it!

I could dig it, dig it, dig it!

That's my thing, far out!'

(singing) Poor caterpillar (end singing).

Did you ever see a catterpillar try to fly before he's got the wings?
  Pitiful.

He couldn't get off the ground.

He took a running start. He was out of shape. He hadn't been
  jogging every day.

He couldn't get up in the sky.

Guess what he said?

He said, 'SCREAM!' Made a lot of noise.

The tree said, 'Don't cry.'

'You are going to be a butterfly,' said the sky, 'That's your destiny.'

He didn't know the word, 'destiny.'

What does the word 'destiny' mean? Tell me.

It's more than what you're looking for. Tell me.

You finally do it. You gonna be that.

He didn't know that word destiny. He had never got to the third
  grade. He had never been to school, he can't read and write. He
  doesn't have a dictionary to look stuff up in at night.

(cry)

Pretty soon he made a little house. What do you call that house?

A little cocoon. He didn't call it a cocoon. He just called it his pad.

Little hip-ity, his tent-city.

It wasn't that pretty. It was dark in there.

Hard to get any air, thought he was gonna die.

He began to cry. Guess what he said?

(scream)

What else?

Guess who heard him scream. What's that round thing in the sky at night?

The moon says, 'Yo, what's happening, bro, que pasa, what it is? Cool it, bro.'

The caterpillar said, 'I don't want to die in the dark, I want to fly.'

The moon said, 'Cool it, baby, cool it. Just hang. Be cool, be cool.'

The moon said, 'Don't you know, God is going to turn you into a beautiful butterfly.'

The caterpillar never heard of God.

He had never been to Sunday School, he had never been to Shabbat.

Never sang those songs.

(cry)

Guess who made him cry? The one who made the sky.

The one that made the pretty green tree.

The one that made pretty you, the one that made raggedy me.

You know who that be.

The boss, the boss!

He said, 'Cool it, I made everything.

I made the sky, I made the river.

I made the tree, I made the tiger.

I make everything.

Don't cry, coochie coo, come on. Come on, don't cry, coochee coo. Don't cry you pretty thing, you. Don't cry, come on. Oh, ah, oh.

Don't you know you're gonna be my butterfly? 'Cause I make stuff.

That's me crying in there.

All you have to do is go for your cry, your dream. The dream is you.

Try with all your might, and guess what? I'm gonna give you those wings. You're gonna be one of those things called butterfly.'

The caterpillar said, 'Far out, wicked, awesome. I could dig it.
Woo-ee, dynamite, outa sight, let's get tight, me and you. Woo
woo! I-tee-a-ee-ee, ooh, ow.' (end of singing)

The sun is rising.

Did you ever watch the sun rise?

The sun rose like this. I'm gonna show you.

The sun got up like this (demonstration with arms outstretched).

The sun rose high in the sky.

The sun was golden, bright, and the sun kissed that cocoon like this:
(kissing sound).

Bright!

Were you ever kissed by the sun? Bright?

Well, inside that cocoon, something felt that kiss. Guess what it was?

Something that was a butterfly is gonna come out.

Inside the cocoon it said, 'Woo-ee, dynamite.' It began to jump
around, scream and shout. It began breakdancing.

Guess what happened?

It broke out.

Something come out of that cocoon, it came out backward, upside
down, breakdancing against the sky.

It was moonwalking on the sun.

Is that cool?

Guess what, when this thing rose, the star said, 'Wow, far out!'

'Wicked awesome,' said the morning lark. 'What are you?'

And this thing said, 'Dig it. I am a butterfly. I am my dream. I am.'

It began to shout, 'Ahhhhhhhhhh, far out.'

So one morning, ah folks; it's so pretty, I can't tell you.

(singing) It was early one morning, oop-a-zee, chuli-bee, oop.

Saul couldn't sit still during this one. The rhythm became so clear that he
'ahhhed' with the caterpillar and made crying sounds and danced all around
to the story.

'I'm a butterfly,' he cried, 'Watch me fly.' And he made a flying leap from the couch to the floor. I could see that this type of story was not calming, but it certainly made him laugh.

During that first session, after he sat down for a few seconds to catch his breath, I asked him about his poor behavior at school. He put his head down and became so quiet it was uncanny. He looked so ashamed.

'Look,' I said, 'I really see that you are a butterfly, that you really do love to fly and that you really are a great kid, and I just want to help you behave so you won't get into trouble anymore. I want you to shed all of that weight so you can really fly!'

'Like this?' he said, suddenly jumping up and leaping all over the room.

'Yes,' I sighed, 'just like that.'

'I don't need no help.'

'You don't?'

'Shit no.'

I was in a junior high school way on the other side of town. Amber Gonzales was a gorgeous, lanky Afro-American 12-year-old. She was already in danger of failing 7th grade, even though she had only been in school for two weeks. School hours were the only time I had to see her. I had a brief phone conversation with her mother, Kareem, who was desperate.

'See my daughter immediately, and then you can come talk with me. She back-talks me, is flunking school, and I am so afraid she's going to end up like me, pregnant at 13 and on drugs. You have got to see her immediately!'

'Can I tell you what your mother said?'

'Fuck her. She don't know nothin'.'

'How come you came out of class with me?'

'My mom told me you was comin' and she'd do nothin' but yell if I didn't.'

'So should I tell Mom you don't want help? I mean I can't force this on you…'

Amber was quiet. She picked up a crayon and began to doodle.

'Is it okay with you if I tell you what Mom said?'

'If you have to.'

I took that as a yes.

'She told me you were failing school.'

'So what the fuck? You know what these fuckin' teachers are like? Everyone's flunkin' out. These stupid teachers don't know how to teach.'

'If you didn't go to school, what would you do?'

'Shit, sing. I'm gonna have me a hip hop band.'

'Do you write your own music?'

Her beautiful brown skin began to turn a shade darker.

'Sometimes.'

'Do write your own lyrics?'

The tension in the room was high.

'Sometimes. Music is the only class I like. My teacher can sing, and she knows good songs and shit.'

'Hmmmm... Do you like poetry?'

'Yeah, sometimes.'

'Can I read you a poetry story here?'

I read Amber *The Butterfly*. I really wasn't sure how it would go over. My rhythm is very different than that of the story, and she really wasn't swaying to it, and it was difficult for me to really read it the way Brother Blue tells it. Afterward Amber said, 'Do you believe that?'

'Do I believe what?'

'That God makes everythin'?'

'Why do you ask?'

'How could He?'

'What do you mean?'

'Shit, don't you know no shit? Do you know how hard my mom works and how many kids she has, and how poor we is, and what an asshole she's with? You think God made all of that?'

'I don't know, Amber. You certainly think very deeply, don't you? Do you really want to know what I think?'

She nodded.

'You know how you can dance and sing and how great you are with rhythm?' She smiled.

'And you saw how I read that story, you know, from my own sense of rhythm?'

Her smile broadened. 'Shit, you have no shit rhythm.'

I could feel myself blushing profusely. 'Well, right. And yet I read that story to you, not to show you how little or how much rhythm I had, but because I knew about your sense of rhythm and I knew you would like it. I think God is about us humans acting honestly and kindly. Do you know what I mean?'

'Like you got embarrassed giving me something so I could like it? You mean like that?'

'Yeah,' I said, 'just like that.'

When you, the therapist, are embarrassed

After reading *The Butterfly* to Amber, a long silence ensued. I became aware of our different outward appearances. I wasn't sure how she would take my help, given how white and unrhythmic I was. I wasn't sure if she would tease me about this or not, and how I would handle it if she did. All I could do, in that moment, was be as honest as I could be with myself. I allowed my own embarrassment of my 'unrhythmic whiteness' to wash over me. As I allowed this to happen, I realized that if I was feeling vulnerable, how must Amber be feeling? The stronger her teasing and protesting, the stronger her vulnerability, far larger than my own.

Note

1 Excerpt from *The Butterfly* by Hugh Morgan Hill (Brother Blue) published in *Talk That Talk* edited by Linda Goss and Marian Barnes (1989) New York: Simon and Schuster. Reproduced with permission of Hugh Morgan Hill.

CHAPTER FOURTEEN

Loss of Gravity

Saul and Rosa kept me waiting for half an hour, as Rosa was on the phone talking with a DSS worker who didn't speak Spanish. Saul was on the other phone translating for Rosa. It was regarding one of the foster children. This was my sixth visit.

It became clear early on that Saul was frustrated and confused. Part of his confusion was around the role he played in the family. This role was similar to the role Andy played in his family (see Part 1). Like Jasmina, Rosa often asked Saul to translate for her. This role of translator was placing Saul in an 'adult' position. First Rosa put him on the phone, asking him to speak to the medical secretary, a foster child's DSS worker, or another professional, and then she was angry with him for not making his bed, helping the other children, cleaning his room, or clearing the table.

By this session, the only other story I had told Saul besides *The Butterfly*, was *How the Bat Came to Be*. This is because Saul wanted to hear the stories over and over. When we finally sat down together this session, he asked me to tell him the story, *How the Bat Came to Be*, for the third time. After the telling of this story Saul said unexpectedly, 'I'm not like that squirrel. She had a lot of friends. I don't have *any* friends. No matter what I do, someone is always trying to hurt me.'

'What do you mean?'

'Well, I hate fighting. That's wrong. Sometimes they call me a girl and I try to walk away and today, well...' His face turned bright red, and he ripped up the drawing he was doing. 'See, I hate fighting, and all my friends want to do is fight. I eat lunch alone; I play alone; I HATE all the fighting and today a kid threw me against the stone wall and I hurt my head.'

'That's awful, Saul. Does your teacher know?'

'They're just really mean. If I told on them, they'd come after me all of the time. You know that squirrel?'

'Yeah?'

'You know how she helped, and then she got blind for helping, but then her wish came true because she helped?'

'Yeah.'

'Does that really happen?'

'What do you think?'

'I don't know.'

'Do you think when things are so bad, you can remember that that sun is always with you, even if you can't feel it?'

'You mean, even though they beat on me, something for me will come true, no matter what?'

'Yes! Exactly. And you know, Saul, you are like that squirrel. I mean, like her, you are really sticking to your belief in what is right, and maybe it's okay to be lonely and mad right now. The squirrel was aware that she was losing her hair, her tail, and her eyesight, but that didn't stop her, right?'

Silence ensued.

'Have you told Mom?' I asked gently.

'She'll get mad.'

'At who?'

'I don't know.'

'Well, you know how all of the animals wanted to protect the squirrel?'

He nodded.

'Maybe you can look at Mom and your teacher like that. They are two people who can help prevent those boys from hurting you. Besides, I think Mom would be happy to help you, and I know your teacher likes you. She just wishes you would listen to her more carefully, and if you're worried about your safety and being lonely, how can you listen?'

Saul was quiet again.

Eventually, he agreed to speak with his parents, who were eating in the kitchen. I met his father for the first time. There was a mile-high pile of rice and pork on his plate. He looked so happy eating. He asked Saul and me to sit down and after a few minutes of awkward small talk, we discussed Saul's problem.

Rosa said, 'You, Saul, have such a heart. You don't have to fight. I will talk with your teacher.'

'Saul,' said his father, 'You are a strong boy. You can beat them up if you want. Don't let them make a girl out of you. But you have to do well in school. Do you understand? You MUST do well in school, no matter what. So if fighting is going to get you in trouble, then beat them up after school, not in the school. If they hurt you in school then report them and get them into trouble. Then they will come for you after school, and I will show you how to defend yourself.'

Rosa stopped him. 'Jesus does not want Saul beating anyone up, you follow? He is too good. I am glad you told me, Saul. It won't happen again. I know most of these boys' parents.' Her eyes were wide and bright. 'They won't touch Saul again, you believe me.' There was something in the way she spoke. You just didn't want to argue. Not any of us.

The clicking of forks and knives reverberated in the silence.

Saul's father stood up. Still chewing, he nodded goodbye, shook my hand, put on his jacket, and left.

I remembered Ricardo's father (see Part 2), and wondered about this man's isolation in the family.

'Where's he going?' I asked.

Rosa shook her shoulders. 'Wherever men go.'

I looked at Saul. The little man left in the house.

Pushing versus accepting

While some work was needed in Rosa's family, I realized that Rosa needed to lean on Saul, and he also needed Rosa. I understood their dynamics, the fluidity and necessity of them, and how impossible they were to change. I was understanding the idea of surrendering.

That's what the squirrel did throughout the story. She surrendered to what she could not control. Her acts were acts of love, and in return, she received her deepest wish: an ability to fly through the nights, with the continuous inner love and compassion from the light, no matter where she went. The truth is that this compassion is always with us. The true 'sacrifice,' I realized, was the personal belief in how things ought to be. Was I witnessing unchanging power plays in this family, or was I witnessing compassion, a surrendering to what neither Rosa nor Saul could control? Was their relationship the power plays I personally believed them to be, or were they, in fact, the very acts of love?

Amber's home was small for the seven people living there. She shared a room with her 11-year-old sister, and her four brothers also shared one room. Her mother, Kareem, worked two jobs and was beginning school the following week. She was gorgeous. She had short cropped hair, walnut brown skin, and huge brown-black eyes with lashes longer than her hair.

'Amber enjoys you,' Kareem was telling me. 'She's always home when you come, and even though she may not say much while she is with you, something is going on, 'cause I'm not gettin' as many calls from her teacher.'

'You know, I been back to school, and I am learnin' 'bout psychology and what happened to me. I been a volunteer as an overnight counselor at a drug re-hab for pregnant teenage girls, and every one of them reminds me of me. I went and done the same thing, and Amber is beautiful, and I ain't been the best example, you know, I only been straight myself for about five or six years now.'

'Congratulations.'

'Yeah, thanks, it's really hard, and I know Amber's been responsible for some things she shouldn't be, but, you know, she don't even wash a dish now and I hate hollerin' at her, but I am so afraid she's gonna be me that I won't let her get away with anythin'.'

'I think Amber hates to be yelled at and I think she feels you're on her case all the time.'

'Oh, I know, but she sees me hollerin' at her sister too.'

'It could be her age, so self-absorbed.'

'Well, that's what I think. I'm just tryin' to get her out of her selfishness.'

Amber must have heard us talking, as she came down the squeaky stairs. She asked me who I was here to see, her mom or her. I was surprised by the question, as Amber really hadn't been saying much to me. Each session I had told her stories or read her poems but there wasn't much conversation.

She led me up to her room. She said, 'Can you read me those poems you read to me last time?'

I read her an untitled poem by Rilke.

Untitled

by Rainer Maria Rilke

You darkness, that I come from,
I love you more than all the fire
that fence in the world,
for the fire makes a circle of light for everyone,
and then no one outside learns of you.

But the darkness pulls in everything;
shapes and fires, animals and myself,
how easily it gathers them! –
powers and people –
and it is possible a great energy
is moving near me.
I have faith in nights.

'That was neat. So like when I don't understand somethin' like that caterpillar, I just have to have faith that I will?'

'Exactly! And you must be already acting on that faith, 'cause Mom says you're doing better in school, are you?'

'She thinks she knows everythin'.'

'Well, she didn't give me the impression she knew everything. She just looked happy and said she wasn't getting any more phone calls from school. I want to know, how come?'

'Well, like I already said. Like that poem. I can have faith in nights and maybe, you know, I'm just a caterpillar right now waitin' to be somethin'.'

And then Amber said she wanted to write a poem.

'What do you want to write about?'

'Flying.'

'What flies and what doesn't fly?'

'Time.'

'Wow, Amber, you go, girl. You are so smart. Go ahead, what's your first line?'

And she wrote the following poem.

Time

by Amber Gonzales

Time flies by as you can see
on the weekend

First one minute then another
then before you know it
almost an hour

When you're sleeping
you feel like you just woke up

When you're watching a TV show end
you feel like it just came on

Look! it's a bird, it's a plane
it's time!

'You really can have faith in your writing,' I said, as I got up to go. 'This is a fun poem.'

'That's what my music teacher says, she says, "You have faith in yourself, and you can go anywhere, no matter what."'

'Smart music teacher.'

'And that's what it says in that poem. Read it once more before you go.'

Once more I read her Rilke's poem. 'I'll make a copy for you and bring it to you next time.'

One week later, in the middle of a Tuesday afternoon, I received an emergency call from Kareem. 'Come over fast, Molly, come over as fast as you can. On the way home from school, Amber, her cousin, and friend were held up at gunpoint. Who knows why? The friend got shot in the arm and was down on the ground, and then Amber was held at gunpoint at her head. The other one, her cousin, ran and got the cops; the boy was caught – a 12-year-old boy wantin' sex and money – and oh, God Jesus, who knows what else! Please come over!'

When I arrived at the house, the entire neighborhood was there, Amber and her cousin were sitting at the table. The support was unbelievable. It was like a funeral or a wedding; there was as much food as there were people, and everyone was talking at once.

Some were going to kill the members of the gunman's family; others were screaming and crying for peace and stronger neighborhood support. My focus was on Kareem, Amber, and her cousin.

I asked Amber to tell the story one more time.

'We was just walkin' home, you know, like we's always does, and this kid comes up and we don't want to walk with him 'cause we just don't. And then he pulls out a gun, and I said, "You got to be kiddin', man" and then he shoots it, and my friend falls down, and then my cousin's runnin' like a horse, and then there's this gun in my head. Then the cops come and an ambulance and the kid runs and my friend goes to the hospital.

'Oh, God, I couldn't stop him, I couldn't stop him, and I even shit in my own pants – oh God, oh my fuckin' God.' Kareem was rubbing her daughter's neck. 'Not your fault, sugar, not your fault. There was nothin' you could do.'

I promised the family I would be back the next day.

That night I couldn't sleep. *How could I help Kareem? What could I do for Amber? What on earth was a little white therapist doing in a job like this?* These thoughts kept me up all night. I thought of Saul, and how easily this could happen to him as well. Was there any protection anywhere?

I wanted to hide under my covers and scream. I suddenly understood how quickly life could become unsafe. I went to my poetry books and I read all of the poems that had ever brought me comfort.

I read Rilke, Mary Oliver, and Rumi. I wrote a poem myself. I decided that I would make packets of poetry for Kareem, Amber, and her cousin, Julie, and her friend, Annie. I didn't know if this would help any of them. All I knew was that these poems brought me great comfort as they talked about the darkness and the struggle and triumph. I did this more for myself than for them. I needed to hand them something that might help, whether it would or not.

I walked into Kareem's house late the next afternoon. Amber and Julie were singing in their room. I spoke with Kareem for a short while and handed her the packet of poems. 'I don't know,' I said, 'these are some of my favorites. I just thought you might like them.'

'Poetry?' She looked at me skeptically.

'Yeah, I love poetry, and so does Amber, and I am going to give these to Amber and Julie. I just thought you would like one too.'

'Thanks.'

'How are you?'

'Sick and tired. Sick and tired. You have no idea. Annie's here too. Thank God. She came out of the hospital this morning with a broken arm. She's alright. Thanks to Jesus! Go on with you, go see Amber, she's waitin' for you.'

When I walked into her room, Amber, Julie, and Annie were singing to a rap song with the lyrics changed to 'Will I live to be 14?'

I sat down on a bed and listened to them sing this song over and over.

A symbiotic relationship

When Amber and her friends sang together in their room, I tried to follow the gist of the song, but rap doesn't move me in the least. Over time, I had grown used to the differences between Amber and me. I was less embarrassed about not liking or understanding things she loved. Amber was so opinionated and so completely sure of her likes and dislikes, that her very opinions helped me form mine more clearly. I wasn't flip-flopping around, trying to be something I wasn't in order to please her, or because I was scared of her. Amber had already had her share of fear and trying to please others, which had created strong defenses in her. Being strong within myself around our differences helped Amber create a more trusting relationship with me.

When the three girls grew tired of singing, I said, 'Look, I have something for you: some poems I put together for you. If you want, I can read the first poem out loud.'

I read the first poem by Rilke. The one that begins: 'Sometimes it is as though I am inside solid stone' (see Part 1).

There was silence at the end.

'It's kinda like you're in so much deep down shit you can't get out,' said Amber.

'That's right, that's it exactly.'

'And maybe you gotta scream real loud to get out.'

'Naaaaa...no matter how much you scream, you never get out of shit.'

No one was much in the mood for writing that day. The girls talked about their experience. Julie didn't say much. She kept reading the poems in the packet. By the end of the session she looked up at me.

'These poems are really cool. How come our teacher don't know about these? Read the last one, that's my favorite.'

The poem was the one I had written.

Untitled

by Molly Salans

Dear Goddess,
There are aches inside aches
unrippling and stuck
they take over my neck
reign in my shoulders

bone boulders

unlike stone
they cannot erode
no matter how many tears
fall in waves around them

I sit within
curled
forgetting how to unwrap
even one letter
toward thought

in such quiet
there is no thing to hear

a cell pulses against my skin
a thin note
of no importance
like one flick of foam
it disappears

I close further
so deeply shut
there is no way through

How is it then
dear Goddess
Your kiss reaches me
in this no space
where there is no room for prayer

How in Your enormity
can You possibly
fit
inside
here?

'That is really cool,' said Julie.
   'What's so cool about it?' asked Amber
   'Well, shit, it's like you can find hope, even in this shithole.'
Silence ensued, and I got up to leave.

A chorus of, 'Thanks, Molly, when you coming' back?' trailed me down the stairs. I saw Kareem smoking her cigarettes, and poring over the packet of poems. I tiptoed out, breathing deeply.

What just happened? I asked myself. Who in the world would have thought that these poems could provide such validation? They certainly held validation for me. Why shouldn't they have an effect on these girls? Why shouldn't they bridge cultures and age and even go beyond? I wondered, could poetry like this be as powerful as their near-death experience?

It was October and the leaves were underfoot. Their crunching sounded exactly like the apple I had just finished eating. I was sitting with Rosa in her kitchen and realizing that another reason for Saul's anxiety was his intense need for perfection.

Rosa was shaking her head. 'The teacher calls me again and again. He won't hand in his work. He erases until he makes the holes in the paper, and then he refuses to hand in his work.'

I nodded. I had noticed this when Saul drew. He often asked for more paper immediately.

'Saul,' I had suggested in one session, 'Make your mistakes into something beautiful. That's what mistakes are for. I mean, look at that caterpillar. He was beautiful just as he was. Only he didn't believe it. Everyone loved him regardless.'

Unwittingly becoming like the parent

Saul refused to draw if I didn't give him new pieces of paper. I thought about holding onto the paper, as I was angry that he wasn't hearing my point. I realized that if I held onto the paper I would have been behaving like his mother and his teacher by resisting his resistance. The anger and frustration I was feeling informed me that I was locked into a power and control battle with Saul. I understood, in that moment, how his mother felt.

This intense frustration also informed me about how Saul was feeling. The issue was not only about me and how deeply annoyed I

> was, it was also about Saul and how frustrated and powerless he was feeling. This realization helped me feel compassion for Saul, his mother, and myself. These thoughts led me away from argument and toward a new way of communicating with him.

As we talked, I was creating a design, and I showed him where I went wrong on the paper. I told him I had made a mistake, and he made a brilliant suggestion as to how to correct it, using the very mistake as material to change the design. When I took his suggestion and created my design, he was impressed. 'Now it's a beautiful flower,' he said.

'Exactly,' I said, 'and this could not have been what it is without that mistake – and a butterfly cannot possibly be a butterfly without being a caterpillar first. Likewise, the squirrel would have never have had wings if she hadn't lost what she *thought* was most precious to her.'

I wondered what this perfectionism was connected with. I wondered what he was defending, what type of fear, or insecurity. I had asked Rosa earlier, 'Does Saul ever defy you here at home?' And she replied, 'He better not, or he'll get the TV turned off. I won't tolerate him talking back to me, that's why I don't understand. He is usually an angel with me. He sponges the table, he plays nicely with his foster brothers, he fights his sister, but only sometimes. He is a good boy. It is only at school.'

The relationship between anxiety, anger, and 'being good'

No one can be 'good' all of the time. All of that anger needs to go somewhere. Saul knew he couldn't get angry at his mother. He was receiving the message that it was bad to be angry. So all of that anger was turning inward toward himself. He was severely self-critical and self-blaming. He was not allowed to 'make a mistake,' or to 'be angry.' He associated anger with mistakes, and therefore both anger and error were intolerable.

As usual, Saul was bouncing all over the sofas. He asked me to tell him *The Butterfly* story for the fourth time. When I had finished reading, I brought up the problem of perfectionism. He just kept drawing. I asked him about his friendships, if things were getting better.

'Sort of. I get teased still 'cause I won't fight.'

'I'm wondering if you're mad at your friends?'

'No.' But his body stiffened and he was coloring harder.

'Is that really true? I mean, teasing can hurt.'

He was silent.

'I just wonder if you would feel better if you got good and mad at your friends.'

'The squirrel didn't get mad, and her wish came true.'

'The caterpillar was mad.'

'It didn't do him no good – everyone told him to calm down.'

'You are right.' Saul was trying to make a relationship to his anger, through story. The caterpillar represented his anxiety, and the squirrel represented 'goodness.'

'You know what I've been thinking about that caterpillar? He wouldn't have gotten anyone's attention if he didn't holler, and sometimes you gotta do that; you know, holler. And I mean holler at the people you're mad at. It is so normal to be angry and to make mistakes. You could say that during the process, the squirrel was making a mistake. I mean, here she is losing everything, and still helping. You could say she was making a big mistake. Yet her very mistake turned into something beautiful. Do you know what I mean?'

He kept drawing. 'I just hate making mistakes, that's all.'

It was time to go. I could tell that Saul was thinking deeply about the stories. Both of them. He knew something was off, although he didn't know what, but I had faith that our conversation was sinking into him like a new story.

CHAPTER FIFTEEN

Northern Lights

It was now April, and the huge, old oaks and the long, thin maples along the common were beginning to bud. The grass was turning green under the melting snow. In spite of the urban setting, the air was fresh and cool, and the scent of blossom was on the wind.

I was with Amber again. She couldn't wait to write poetry.

'I do think I'm gonna be somethin'.'

'How, Amber? It seems like you're still doing poorly in school.'

'You know, I keep thinkin' 'bout what happened to me, and I keep thinkin', like you say, "How come I'm alive?" And am I really gonna be somethin' like that story? And school is so fuckin' stupid.'

'How's about if I read you another poem?'

She agreed.

Untitled
by Rumi

Beyond the right and the wrong of things
there is a field
I'll meet you there

When the soul lies down in that grass
the world is too full to talk about
and even the words 'each other'
don't make any sense

'Okay. It's my turn to write one now.'

'What do you want to write about?'

'I'm so tired all of the time, and I get really sleepy in school – it's so fuckin' borin'.'

I'm Tired, I'm Tired

by Amber Gonzales

I'm tired I'm tired
I want to lie down
I want to sleep
and have sweet sweet dreams

But I am in school
my eyes droop down
my shoulders sag
I walk real slow

Lord help me Lord help me
I want to sleep
and have sweet sweet dreams

'That was fun.'

'You're wide awake.'

'Well, yeah, you don't have to go to no school to write.'

'How did you learn to write?'

'School. But that ain't the fuckin' point. I know how to write. I know I wants to sing and write – I don't need no fuckin' school. I'm only here for my friends.'

'What is it that's so awful about school, Amber?'

'I hate my fuckin' teachers.'

'Why?'

'They's borin'.'

'Are they boring, or are they teaching difficult subjects? Is school really hard for you, or is it really boring?'

About boredom

Often when kids tell me something is boring, it turns out that the subject matter or the situation is really hard. Boring is a way to avoid feeling the hardship of things. I knew how hard Amber's life was and I wondered whether the question about school being boring or difficult was too direct. I knew that anger was her defense, and that beneath her rage she was sensitive and vulnerable. She didn't know how to handle these sensitivities yet, although story and poetry were helping.

While she was still yelling at her mother I had to assume she wouldn't treat her teachers any differently. Or myself, for that matter. By trying to help her create a relationship to her hardships, I hoped she would have better ways of handling her pain, when the angry defense was peeled off. This was indeed what her poem was saying. Amber was exhausted on all levels and her dream was to have her life be sweet.

'It's borin' shit. You don't get it, do you?'

'Maybe I don't, Amber. I mean, here you just wrote a poem about how tired you are and how school makes you fall asleep. I do know that your life has been hard, though. I mean, what happened to you a few weeks ago was pretty scary. Remember that poem your cousin liked so much?'

'You mean, that no matter how shitty your life is, there is still hope?'

'Yes. And you can only find that hope when you really face how hard your life is.'

'Then you're not fake like my stupid teacher, Mrs White. I'm gonna write about her right now.'

Patience in therapy

At many of her sessions, Amber really wasn't ready to face herself:
all of her fears, and anger, and pain, and all of the times she had seen
her mother hurting and heartbroken over the boyfriend she was
still with. Amber was so defenseless, and she needed time to absorb
the tragedies she had seen. I needed to go slowly, and hold the
understanding I had of her. Talking about her life would not help,
as she frequently demonstrated. She was, at the moment, learning to
express her anger creatively, and that was already a new way of
dealing with pain. I needed to be careful I wouldn't miss the steps
she was taking quite rightly on her own.

I also needed to consider that I had entered her family system so
much, and that by developing this new trust we had, I was
becoming like her mother: wanting her to understand things in
order to help her avoid further suffering. I had to acknowledge that
rather than protecting her, I was avoiding facing the pain between
us and how helpless I felt consciously watching her suffer.

Mrs White, the Devil (my teacher)
by Amber Gonzales

She's the devil in hell
she's hell on earth
her cheeks are flabby
she's almost bald
her mouth sags down too

She throws hard words
that can break your heart.

'Amber, I'm really sorry you have such an awful teacher. I mean, if she really
is this harsh, how can you possibly learn from her?'

'I told you. Shit, I told you, you don't get much.'

'Has she broken your heart?'

'I don't want to miss music.'

I looked at the clock. We had some time left, and I told her this.

'Has she broken your heart?' I asked again.

Amber shrugged. 'She's just really mean.'

'You've had enough meanness in your life, huh? I'm really glad you wrote this poem – you express yourself so beautifully and clearly.'

'Yeah.'

'How are things with Mom?'

'All she does is yell for no reason.'

'That's funny, that's what she says you do!'

'Yeah, well, she fuckin' starts it.'

This wasn't getting anywhere.

'Does Mrs White remind you of your mother?'

'Hell, no, shit. Mom ain't mean – she just don't know shit. Mrs White, shit, she's a fuckin' devil. But I'm gonna be somethin' 'cuz like that poem says, I can have faith in black, 'cuz I am black, that's what Mom says.'

'What a wise mother you have.'

It was May 1999, and I had just given notice at my job, for many reasons and it was time for me to devote more time to the part-time private practice I had begun one year before. It was my last session with Amber. I met her at home, and she immediately wanted to look at the poems I had given her in that packet.

She was particularly struck by Rilke's poem about being stuck inside solid stone.

'What if I'm always bad? What if I decide to be bad instead of good?'

'Don't you think you have both? And I'm not sure what you mean by bad and good.'

'Mom says all the time, "I'm afraid you's gonna come to no good, I wish you would do your chores and your homework instead of yellin' and cussin' all the time." But what if I was really like that?'

'What if you were?'

Amber was already trying to tell me a poem. This is what she wrote during that last session.

I'll be Nasty and Bad

by Amber Gonzales

I'll do every bad thing there is
pull all the clothes out of my drawer
pull the pictures down from the wall
won't clean my room anymore
won't listen to my mom anymore
I won't be good anymore.

'I don't really mean this. I mean I just feel like I can't do nothin' right with Mom hollerin' all the time.'

'Why does she yell at you so much?'

"Cause she loves me.'

'Because she loves you?'

'Yeah, she threw asshole out [the boyfriend]. She was screamin' so fuckin' loud "GET OUT GET OUT GET OUT." He was swingin' at her, I was scared and my littlest sister was hidin' under this here bed, and Mom said somethin' 'bout the police, and then the door slammed so hard it shook the house and he ain't been back. Mom said she did it 'cause she loves us and she's tired, so tired, of bein' stuck under a rock.'

'Amber, what do you think about all of this?'

'Finally, she did somethin' for herself, you know?'

'Yeah?'

'An' she's back doin' her homework, you know? An' she got a call from some agency. I think she has some job helpin' pregnant teens. Shit, men are shit. She don't have to worry 'bout me, I ain't gonna fuck no one. I ain't gonna be like her. I'm gonna be somethin' like that butterfly.'

I saw Amber's mother one year later, when I asked her to sign the permission forms allowing me to publish Amber's poems.

'I can't wait to see them in print. She made the honor roll this year, and you should see the songs she's writin'! And I'm workin' with pregnant teens. Oohwee, what a life, eh, Molly? Oh, by the way, you know those poems you gave us a long time ago? I keep them with me. Thanks.'

I gave Kareem a hug, thanking all of the poets who had ever given me hope, and thanking Amber and her mom for their courage to face their struggles.

I was with Saul again. His mother said that things were improving. She was sorry that I was leaving the agency, and she thanked me profusely for helping Saul. His behavior in school was improving daily, although his problems with loneliness and perfectionism were still standing in his way.

When we were once again seated in the living room, he asked to hear *The Butterfly* one more time. This time as I read, Saul hollered with the caterpillar as he was just dying to become a butterfly, danced with the moon and the sun as they tried to soothe the poor caterpillar, and jumped up and down when God himself entered to teach the caterpillar. By the end of the story, Saul was hopping, skipping, and singing around the room. He said to me, 'When I make mistakes, my heart hurts...' and by the end of that session he had created the poem *Special*.

Special
by Saul Veracruz

When I make mistakes
my heart hurts
to go to sleep
and dream
and make stories in my brain
and then my heart feels like I'm riding a horse

My light is special
My light lives in my special heart

I always make mistakes
and my heart always cries
I make stories when I close my eyes
The light in my heart never dies

'Saul, this is incredible.'

'I love to make stories and pictures!'

'And you love to hear stories!'

And once again we discussed this story, as well as *How the Bat Came to Be*. They were both about animals flying in the end. They were both about faith, no matter how dark things became.

'The caterpillar and the squirrel have millions of friends. And there's no one mean in any of those stories.'

'You're right,' I said. 'The caterpillar and the squirrel have to rely on that "thing" which never dies in order to make their most desired wish come true. And that thing which never dies is inside you and me. It's inside the people you don't like, and it's even inside the very mistakes you make.'

As we were talking, Saul was drawing a picture to his poem.

Figure 14. 'Special' by Saul Veracruz

He suddenly looked up at me excitedly. He pointed to the heart which he had just drawn. 'Looks like a butterfly, look, Molly, a butterfly heart!' On one side of the heart he wrote 'mistakes' and on the other side of the heart he wrote 'stories.'

When I returned for the last few sessions, Saul reported each time that he had a friend, 'who doesn't fight.'

'Really?' I said.

'Yeah, he just came up to me and we started playing and then he played with me a lot. And he told me that he hates fighting.'

'Saul, that's great. I am so happy for you.'

'Yeah.'

'How do you think that happened?'

'I hate to fight.'

'Yeah. And how did you meet this friend, when you were so sure you wouldn't?'

'I don't know. The caterpillar and the squirrel have millions of friends. Why can't I have just one? And that thing that never dies, well, the caterpillar became a butterfly with that, and the squirrel became a bat with that! Why can't I have just one friend?'

'Well, absolutely.' I was utterly speechless. After some silence, I said, 'Your mom tells me that you're handing in your homework.'

'I am.' He looked up from his drawing and beamed at me.

'How come?'

'I just am. I try to tell myself that I am something, even if I don't know that yet.'

As I drove away from Saul's home, knowing I would see him only one more time, I was once again amazed at the power of story and poetry.

Saul, the caterpillar and the squirrel

Saul had deeply identified with the caterpillar. He, like the caterpillar, was dying to 'become' something, but he had no idea what. Like the caterpillar, he expressed anxiety by calling out of turn: not listening, and insisting on unreasonable perfection. Those who encouraged Saul – his teacher, mother, therapist – were akin to the sun, the moon, and the trees in the story who tried to help the caterpillar. Like these characters, the people supporting Saul kept telling him to relax, to calm down. He certainly would become something special. In addition, Saul *knew*, just like those supporting the caterpillar, that the caterpillar would become a butterfly. By analogy, the 'something that never dies, the something that is God' opened deep inside Saul, allowing him, unconsciously, to know that he, too would and could transform.

In addition, the story *How the Bat Came to Be* deepened his conviction that he truly could transform. This story confirmed his deep sense of compassion, which guided him innately away from violent interactions. All of this led to his poem *Special*, and consequently to his improved behavior. As his mother said after reading the poem, 'Ay, Dios, que corazon, que corazon!' (Oh, God, what a heart, what a heart!) I couldn't agree more.

Saul had found his own inner light, and could shine like the star he was. He certainly did reach out and take one star, the only star he could: his own – as had all of the children I had worked with over this five-year period. In watching them create their own unique selves, they humbled and taught me deeper and deeper meanings of hope and possibility. I am indebted to these children, and when I gaze up at the sky at night and see those sparkling stars, I am reminded of how many stars I have come in contact with, and how lucky I was to do so.

References

Barks, C. (trans) (1997) *The Essential Rumi.* San Francisco: John Moyne Harpur.

Botkins, O. (1977) *The Museletter 10, 2,* LANES (Lanes for Advancement of New England Storytellers).

Bowen, M. and Kerr, M. E. (1998) *Family Evaluation: An Approach Based on Bowen Theory.* New York: W. W. Norton & Company.

Brother Blue, *The Butterfly* from L. Goss and M. Barnes (eds) (1989) *Talk That Talk.* New York: Simon and Schuster.

Caduto, M. J. and Bruchac, J. (1994) *Keepers of the Night: Native American Stories and Nocturnal Activities for Children.* Golden, CO: Fulcrum Publishing.

Eliach, Y. (1982) *A Girl Called Estherke* from *Hasidic Tales of the Holocaust.* New York: Vintage Books.

Estes, C.P. (1997) *Storytelling Magazine,* July, 14.

Gillard, M. (1996) *Storyteller, Storyteacher.* York, Maine: Stenhouse Publishers.

Hughes, L. (1994) *Stars* from A. Rampersad (ed) *The Collected Poems of Langston Hughes.* New York: Alfred A. Knopf.

Pearmain, E. D. (1999) *Doorways to the Soul.* The Pilgrim Press.

Phelps, E. J. (1981) *The Maid of the North: Feminist Folk Tales From Around The World.* New York: Henry Holt and Company.

Rilke, R.M. (1981) *Selected Poems of Rainer Maria Rilke.* Translated by Robert Bly. New York: Harper and Row Publishers.

Rosman, S. M. (1989) *A Most Precious Gift* from *Sidrah Stories: A Torah Companion.* New York: UAHC Press.

Vuong, L. D. (1982) *The Fairy Grotto* from *The Brocaded Slipper and Other Vietnamese Tales.* London: HarperCollins Juvenille Books.

Index